WHAT IF . . .

Collected
Thought Experiments
in Philosophy

Peg Tittle

PEARSON
Longman

New York San Francisco Boston
London Toronto Sydney Tokyo Singapore Madrid
Mexico City Munich Paris Cape Town Hong Kong Montreal

Vice President and Publisher: Priscilla McGeehon
Executive Marketing Manager: Ann Stypuloski
Managing Editor: Bob Ginsberg
Project Coordination, Text Design, and Electronic Page Makeup:
    Sunflower Publishing Services
Cover Design Manager: John Callahan
Cover Designer: Sunflower Publishing Services
Cover Image: Corbis/Bettman, Inc.
Manufacturing Buyer: Roy L. Pickering, Jr.
Printer and Binder: RR Donnelley & Sons Company
Cover Printer: Coral Graphic Services

Library of Congress Cataloging-in-Publication Data
Tittle, Peg 1957–
    What if— : collected thought experiments in philosophy / Peg Tittle.
      p. cm.
    Includes bibliographical references and index.
    ISBN 0-321-20278-3
    1. Thought experiments.   I. Title.

BD265.T57 2005
100—dc22   2004044439

Please visit our website at http://www/ablongman.com

ISBN 0-321-20278-3

12345678910—DOH—06050403

CONTENTS

PREFACE

This book was initially conceived as a handy reference for philosophers of all kinds ("That thing about Mary, the neuroscientist who's color-blind or something—where is it? who's it by?"—not to worry—Mary's in here. So's the brain in a vat, the bat, the violinist, the teletransporter . . .).

However, it soon became apparent what a great introduction to philosophy this would be, both for ordinary people (think of it as gourmet food for thought—when TV becomes junk food that doesn't really satisfy, try a few of these) and for students (yes, they would be your nonordinary people): thought experiments are such delightful door openers—and you can walk around for hours behind those doors and not be bored, the detail is so rich (and that's *before* you get lost). And since it seems that those working in ethics are particularly fond of thought experiments, the book may be a good supplement in ethics courses as well as introductory philosophy courses.

In fact, this book may, more than traditional philosophy texts, achieve some standard pedagogical objectives: awaken intellectual curiosity, because each thought experiment presents a puzzling, and sometimes addictively intriguing, situation that demands a response; demonstrate that philosophy is valuable, because many of these thought experiments address a genuine problem in life, despite appearing to be quite off-the-wall; and initiate students into the disciplined kind of thought required by philosophy, because in the course of working out their response, students will learn how to think clearly and coherently. And who knows, someone might be so intrigued by which way James walks home (see "James's Way Home") or whether Jill knows that the political leader has been assassinated (see "Harman's False Report") she or he will decide to pursue a degree in philosophy, establish a career in metaphysics or epistemology. . . .

As for deciding what to include (and what not), rather than adhere to some particular definition, I have often used effect as my guide: if the scenario seems to serve "merely" to illustrate or clarify a point—that is, people will probably read it, understand the point being made, and move on—then I have tended not to include it; however, if, for some reason, the scenario seems to be a showstopper—that is, people will probably read it, pause, reflect on it, wrestle with it, and discuss it—if it seems to be truly *thought-provoking*—then I have tended to include it.

Since this is a book intended to be a reference, I have included the scenarios people might most expect to find in such a book, the bits and pieces philosophers have come to consider as thought experiments—even though by some definitions some of these may not actually be thought experiments.

And since the book is also intended to be a course text, I have included, along with the "classics," some "should-be classics." I have also tried to include a fair number from each of the many fields and time periods in philosophy—though it seems thought experiments are simply far more prevalent in some fields and time periods than in others.

In the interests of keeping the book compact and affordable, I have excluded the categories of science and literature. That is to say, experiments addressing a scientific question (such as Schrödinger's Cat and the many thought experiments conducted by ancient philosophers, when philosophy was early science) and experiments that appear in literary material are not included. Certainly many matters of science are philosophical in nature and many works of literature have great philosophical value (utopian and dystopian novels, for example, can be considered extended thought experiments), but I had to draw a line somewhere! For the same reason, I have severely limited the number of philosophical paradoxes I've included.

I have used rather broad categories in the table of contents so one can see, at a glance, the breadth of the book. However, for more specific purposes, I have also organized the thought experiments by author, date, and keyword/subject (see the indexes at the back).

As for ordering the experiments within categories, rather than agonize over various equally good arrangements, I decided to order them by chronology. Readers can go wherever and whenever their curiosities take them, and instructors can select and order to fit their purposes. Hopefully, the indices at the back and the many cross-references within the commentaries will help in this regard.

While it is certainly possible, and valuable, to have fun with the thought experiments just as they appear, I have provided a short commentary for each that highlights the important elements of the experiment, summarizes the context out of which the experiment was taken, and suggests the larger context in which the experiment arises. I have also included a few thought-provoking questions of my own.

For further thought provocation, one can consult the many articles written about pretty much every thought experiment in here. A quick search in *The Philosophers' Index* or on any of the many philosophy search websites, using the author's name and key words in the title of the experiment, should yield several inviting possibilities.

Thanks, first and foremost, to all the philosophers who came up with these delightfully engaging scenarios! Thanks also to the many people (especially reviewers, but also members of the philosophical community at large) for suggestions and feedback, including the following: Jared Bates, Indiana University Southeast; John Bouseman, Hillsborough Community College; Ron Cooper, Central Florida Community College; Robert Hood, Middle Tennessee State University; Keith Korcz, University of Louisiana at Lafayette; Augustine M. Nguyen, University of Louisville; Kelly A. Parker, Grand Valley State University; Craig Payne, Indian Hills College; Philip Pecorino, Queensborough Community College; Christopher Robertson, Washington University in St. Louis; David A. Salomon, Black Hills State University; Edward Schoen, Western Kentucky University; Samuel Thorpe, Oral Roberts University; Ted Toadvine, Emporia State University; Mike VanQuikenborne, Everett Community College; W. Steve Watson, Bridgewater College; Steve Young, McHenry County College; and David Yount, Maricopa University. Thanks, lastly, to Priscilla McGeehon and Pearson Longman.

PEG TITTLE

INTRODUCTION

So what exactly *is* a thought experiment? Broadly speaking, and as the title of the book suggests, it's a "what if?"—conducting a thought experiment is engaging in hypothetical reasoning. Like a regular experiment, a thought experiment involves setting up a situation and then paying close attention to what happens. Unlike regular experiments, however, thought experiments are conducted in the laboratory of the mind. So the situations are imaginary—often *very* imaginary.

Nevertheless, like regular experiments, thought experiments are "what-ifs" with a purpose—so much so that the line between illustrative example and thought experiment can become a little fuzzy. Many experiments "simply" demonstrate a point—after all, the designers have done their homework and have a pretty good idea about what, given the situation they describe, will happen. In these cases, the interesting part is figuring out the implications, the meaning, of what happens.

In addition to making a point, however, thought experiments often do one or more of the following:

- ask a question
- answer a question
- reveal an inconsistency in our thinking
- reveal a lack of clarity in our thinking
- lead us to reconsider, revise, or refine our thinking
- display something puzzling (which may then lead us to think or rethink . . .)
- support a claim, view, hypothesis, or theory
- undermine a claim, view, hypothesis, or theory
- test the adequacy of a definition
- test the applicability of a principle

This list is not intended to be exhaustive—thought experiments most certainly do other things as well (annoy, amuse, perplex, disturb, fascinate . . .)—but it's a good starting point. (And figuring out what, exactly, the thought experiment *is* intended to do is a good way to start thinking about it.)

A common reaction to thought experiments is that they're "too far-fetched"—what's described could never or would never happen. And that's often true. But thought experiments are not intended to describe what could or would happen. Whether something is *conceptually possible* is different from whether something is *actually possible*. And usually what's being investigated in thought experiments is the stuff in our conceptual realm—our ideas, our thoughts and opinions, *about* what may or may not happen. And stuff in our conceptual realm is *independent* from stuff in our physical realm; for example, what we think about blind dogs who chase bright green tennis balls is independent from whether they actually exist or are likely to exist. (Further, and more generally speaking, just because something doesn't exist or hasn't happened doesn't mean it's irrelevant to us—what will happen in the future has not yet happened and so does not yet exist, but it's still important to us.) As Tamar Gendler notes, it is somewhat surprising that "thinking about what there isn't and how things aren't" should help us to learn about what there is and how things are" (*Thought Experiment: On the Powers and Limits of Imaginary Cases,* New York: Garland Press, 2000, 1)—but it does. It also helps us learn about how things *should* be; indeed, that something could never or would never actually happen doesn't change its moral rightness or wrongness—so far-fetchedness turns out to be irrelevant. Furthermore, it may be that at least in ethics, as Jonathan Dancy argues, imaginary scenarios are as good as real ones for helping us decide what we should do: "If we find that our past experience is . . . no guide or insufficient guide, we can let ourselves be guided instead by cases made up for the purpose" ("The Role of Imaginary Cases in Ethics," *Pacific Philosophical Quarterly* 66 [Jan–Apr 1985]: 141–153, 142).

Another common reaction is to declare that the experiment doesn't provide enough information for us to answer the question posed. Fair enough. But the experiment can still be useful: by figuring out exactly what information is needed, one is identifying the relevant factors with regard to the question at hand. And that's important. It's also valuable, and interesting, to figure out what changes in what bits of information would change our answers.

Yet another criticism (mostly with regard to thought experiments in ethics and personal identity) is that the "findings" of the experiment can't justifiably be applied to the real world. Also fair enough. Perhaps the experiment has been poorly designed and critical elements have been omitted, or delineated in such a way as to "nullify" the results or limit their applicability.

Can thought experiments fail? Certainly. One way in which an experiment can fail is if, as just mentioned, it can't be applied as intended. Another way it can fail is if it's incoherent—that is, if the terms of the experiment are contradictory, if the scenario itself doesn't "make sense." Yet another way an experiment can fail is if there are errors in the reasoning of the underlying argument.

Thought experiments can be deceptive because they often seem to have a careless, "anything goes" air about them, but don't be misled: they must be approached with the same disciplined and rigorous thought required by philosophical inquiry in less fanciful contexts.

That said, have fun with what you find here!

(You may even want to design your own thought experiment—what if. . . .)

WHAT IF...

ZENO'S ACHILLES

Imagine a race between a runner named Achilles and a tortoise. The tortoise is given a head start of some distance, and they both start at the same time. Achilles must, of course, first cover the distance between the starting line and the tortoise's starting point, but during that time the tortoise will have moved ahead a bit; then Achilles must cover the distance between the tortoise's starting point and the point to which the tortoise has moved, during which time the tortoise will have moved ahead a bit further; and so on and so on. Whenever Achilles reaches the point at which the tortoise was, the tortoise will have moved a bit further ahead, so though Achilles will continue to narrow the distance between himself and the tortoise, he will never catch up to the tortoise. But surely that can't be right!

Furthermore, tortoise or no tortoise, Achilles will never reach the finish line for the same reason. How can that be?

Further still, before he can cover the whole distance, he must cover the first half; before he covers the first half, he must cover the first half of that; and so on. In fact, it looks like Achilles might not even get started!

Source: Attributed to Zeno, c. 500 BCE, by Aristotle. Original articulation of the problem not available; this is a composite of several contemporary articulations.

Zeno's paradoxes (there are several) inquire into the nature of space, time, motion, continuity, and infinity. This one seems to show that motion is impossible. Or does it merely show that basic mathematics (arithmetic and geometry) can't account for motion through time and space? (Or has Zeno simply not correctly accounted for the difference in speed or, as Lewis Carroll suggests, for the fact that the distances to be covered by Achilles are constantly diminishing in length?) Can the paradox be explained with contemporary math (calculus) and physics? If so, does that mean contemporary math and physics defy logic—or the world as we know it (in which Achilles would certainly finish the race)?

The paradox seems to arise only because reality is divided into separate parts (as advocated, for example, by the Pythagoreans). So does Zeno's thought experiment prove, as he intended, that reality is singular and unchanging (as advocated, for example, by Parmenides)? (See "Shoemaker's Time-Freezing World.") Or does it, as some philosophers suggest, show that reality contains contradictions?

Perhaps the problem is inherent in the experiment itself. It postulates an infinite sequence of actions (covering half the distance, then half again, then half again), then suggests it odd that a finite action (reaching the finish line) can't be achieved. Given the terms, is that so odd? Especially when that finite action is set at the outermost boundary of the infinite series? That is, if the point from which the first half had been calculated is set elsewhere—specifically, at a point equidistant *past* the finish line—then Achilles *would* finish. (Wouldn't he?)

Then again, an infinite journey is not the same as an infinite number of journeys. It's not the *distance* between points A and B that's infinite, but the *number of times that distance can be divided*. So might Achilles complete the finite journey from starting line to finish line and, in so doing, complete the infinite number of journeys in between (the half journey, the quarter journey, the eighth journey, and so on)? (Would *that* be a paradox?)

Perhaps there is a confusion here between logical possibility and physical possibility. For surely, *logically* speaking, if Achilles can do "X" (run from one point to another), he can do "X + 1" (run from that point to yet another), and so on. Then again, even logically speaking, how can he complete (that is, come to the end of) an infinite sequence of tasks—doesn't "infinite" *mean* "without end"?

L<small>UCRETIUS'S</small> S<small>PEAR</small>

[I]f we should theorize that the whole of space were limited, then if a man ran out to the last limits and hurled a flying spear, would you prefer that, whirled by might and muscle, the spear flew on and on, as it was thrown, or do you think something would stop and block it?

Source: Lucretius. *De Rerum Natura.* Book I: 968–973. c. 95–55 BCE. Frank O. Copley, trans. New York: W. W. Norton, 1977. 23–24.

Part of a larger discussion about the nature of reality, this thought experiment leads Lucretius to conclude that space is infinite: on the one hand, if the spear hits a barrier or an edge, Lucretius reasoned, then there must be something beyond that edge, so space is infinite ("There can be no end to anything without something beyond to mark that end" [960–961]); on the other hand, if it doesn't hit a barrier and the spear goes on forever, then, again, space is infinite.

Is there something wrong with Lucretius's thought experiment? How can opposite results lead to the same conclusion? Or must his conclusion that space is infinite be accepted?

Berkeley's Impossibility of Conceiving the Unconceived

But, say you, surely there is nothing easier than for me to imagine trees, for instance, in a park, or books existing in a closet, and nobody by to perceive them. . . . But do not you yourself perceive or think of them all the while? This therefore is nothing to the purpose; it only shews you have the power of imagining or forming ideas in your mind: but it doth not shew that you can conceive it possible the objects of your thought may exist without the mind. To make out this, it is necessary that you conceive them existing unconceived or unthought of. . . . But . . . the mind . . . is deluded to think it can and doth conceive bodies existing unthought of or without the mind.

Source: George Berkeley. *Of the Principles of Human Knowledge.* 1710. As reprinted in *The English Philosophers from Bacon to Mill.* Edwin A. Burtt, ed. New York: Random House, 1939. 509–579. 530.

According to Berkeley, the result of this thought experiment—our inability to conceive of something that is unconceived—is sufficient proof against the existence of material substance. Hence his famous *esse est percipi*—"to be is to be perceived." It's not that trees and books and such disappear when we leave the room (though how would we know?)—they were never there as physical objects in the first place. (If a tree falls in the forest and there's no one around to hear it, does it make a sound? What tree?) When we perceive an object, Berkeley says, we're not really experiencing the object itself—we're experiencing only our sensations. "A cherry," for example, "is nothing but a congeries of sensible impressions, or ideas perceived by various senses, which ideas are united into one thing (or have one name given them) by the mind because they are observed to attend each other . . . take away the sensations of softness, moisture, redness, tartness, and you take away the cherry" *(Three Dialogues Between Hylas and Philonous)*. The fact that an object can seem both small and large depending on how far away from it you are (or that water can seem both warm and cool depending on how hot or cold your hand is when you immerse it) suggests further that the object itself has no definite intrinsic quality; so we can't, and shouldn't, postulate that it actually—physically, materially—exists. Thus, Berkeley refutes materialism (the view that objects exist external to us, in space), advocating instead immaterialism.

But *is* it impossible to conceive the unconceived? And if so, does that prove objects don't physically exist? If you take away the sensations, *do* you take away the cherry—or just the experience of the cherry?

Further, how is it, one might ask, that we all seem to have the same sensations at the same time—say, when we all walk into the wall that's not really there? Berkeley's answer is that there's a god that makes it so. Postulating such a god is, to his mind, more reasonable than postulating the existence of material objects. Is it? Why? (Or why not?) And what are the moral implications for this god, and for us, if this is so—that is, if there is some god putting all our ideas into our head?

Nietzche's Eternal Recurrence

What if some day or night a demon were to steal after you into your loneliest loneliness and say to you: "This life as you now live it and have lived it, you will have to live once more and innumerable times more; and there will be nothing new in it, but every pain and every joy and every thought and sigh and everything unutterably small or great in your life will have to return to you, all in the same succession and sequence—even this spider and this moonlight between the trees, and even this moment and I myself. The eternal hourglass of existence is turned upside down again and again, and you with it, speck of dust!"

Would you not throw yourself down and gnash your teeth and curse the demon who spoke thus? Or have you once experienced a tremendous moment when you would have answered him: "You are a god and never have I heard anything more divine!"

Source: Friedrich Nietzsche. *The Gay Science.* Section 341. 1882. Walter Kaufmann, trans. New York: Random House, 1974. 273.

While the possibility of eternal recurrence—a rather special sort of infinity—is considered by most to be (merely) an intriguing "what-if?" motivating an examination of one's life, Nietzsche actually considered it to be "the most *scientific* of all hypotheses" (*The Will to Power*, note 55) because it follows from the denial of a god: (1) if there is no god, there is no creation or beginning, and, therefore, time is infinite; (2) the number of things and arrangements of things is finite; therefore, (3) events must repeat themselves, infinitely—hence, eternal recurrence. (Is that argument sound?)

Nietzsche expects that most people would be appalled to discover they had to live their life over and over and over again, and indeed Nietzsche himself considered eternal recurrence to be at first glance horrible. However, denying eternal recurrence is a sign of weakness, Nietzsche says, whereas accepting it requires a certain courage and strength, to say "Yes!" to life as it is, with its pain as well as its joys.

Furthermore, he says, "The question in each and every thing, 'Do you desire this once more and innumerable times more?'" (section 341) will either crush you *or* lead you to transform your life—what if one were to live life *as if* it were to recur eternally?

(Of course, if you've looked at some of the other experiments in this collection, you'll say, "Wait a minute—will I *know* my life is happening again and again?")

STRAWSON'S NO-SPACE WORLD

What does the suggestion that we explore [a] No-Space world amount to? What is it to imagine ourselves dispensing with outer sense? . . . The only objects of sense-experience would be sounds. Sounds of course have temporal relations to each other, and may vary in character in certain ways: in loudness, pitch and timbre. But they have no intrinsic spatial characteristics. . . . I shall take it as not needing further argument that in supposing experience to be purely auditory, we are supposing a No-Space world. . . .

The question we are to consider, then, is this: could a being whose experience was purely auditory have a conceptual scheme which provided for objective particulars?

Source: P. F. Strawson. *Individuals.* Garden City, NY: Anchor Books, 1959. 56–58.

S trawson states that in *Individuals,* he is engaging in "descriptive metaphysics"—"describing the actual structure of our thought about the world" (xiii). "We think of the world as containing particular things some of which are independent of ourselves" (2), Strawson says, and we seem to accord special importance to their spatiotemporal position. Why is that so? He replies that "the system of spatiotemporal relations has a peculiar comprehensiveness and pervasiveness, which qualify it uniquely to serve as the framework within which we can organize our individuating thought about particulars" (13). Every particular thing seems to have its place in this system, which makes it easy to identify them, to refer to them, to communicate with each other about them. However, Strawson suggests, other conceptual schemes could exist; materiality (spatiotemporal position) is not a necessary condition of objective particulars. And his No-Space world is intended to demonstrate such an alternative scheme.

One might raise the objection that sound is, in fact, spatial—doesn't it come from the right or left, from near or far? Yes, Strawson would reply, but this seems so only because we have our other space-based senses (such as touch); if we had *only* auditory sense, sounds wouldn't seem spatially located.

Would sounds be identifiable particulars in his No-Space world, as he claims (for he answers his question with a "yes")? That is, if there were nothing else but sound, how could the beings in that world distinguish between them and not-them? Strawson replies that audible continuity or discontinuity could be used as a criterion.

Another interesting question is whether, given that there is no spatial sense at all (for the beings themselves or for the things in their world), such beings would be able to distinguish between themselves and the sounds—or for that matter, between themselves and other selves? If so, how so?

QUINTON'S TWO-SPACE MYTH

[S]uppose that your dream-life underwent a remarkable change. Suppose that on going to bed at home and falling asleep, you found yourself to all appearances waking up in a hut raised on poles at the edge of a lake. A dusky woman, whom you realize to be your wife, tells you to go out and catch some fish. The dream continues with the apparent length of an ordinary human day, replete with an appropriate and causally coherent variety of tropical incident. At last you climb up the rope ladder to your hut and fall asleep. At once you find yourself awaking at home, to the world of normal responsibilities and expectations. The next night life by the side of the tropical lake continues in a coherent and natural way from the point at which it left off. Your wife says "You were very restless last night. What were you dreaming about?" and you find yourself giving her a condensed version of your English day. And so it goes on. Injuries given in England leave scars in England, insults given at the lakeside complicate lakeside personal relations. One day in England, after a heavy lunch, you fall asleep in your armchair and dream of yourself, or find yourself, waking up in the middle of the night beside the lake. Things get too much for you at the lakeside, your wife has departed with all the cooking-pots, and you suspect that she is urging the villagers to sacrifice you to the moon. So you fall on your fish-spear and from that moment on your English slumbers are disturbed no more than in the old pre-lakeside days.

Is such a two-space reality conceivable? That is, is it conceivable that we could live in two different but real spaces?

Source: Anthony Quinton. "Spaces and Times." *Philosophy* 37 (1962): 130–147. 141.

Quinton is investigating with this thought experiment the commonly held notion that space and time are unitary—that is, that we take (and according to Kant, are *compelled* to take) "real spatial extents and temporal durations to be part of the one space and the one time" (139). Wondering whether there are any conceivable circumstances in which it would be reasonable to revise that notion, Quinton presents his Two-Space Myth and shows that it *is* conceivable that we could live in two different but real spaces. Quinton argues that the lake life is just as coherent as the life in England, and it could be just as public (the lake villagers confirm your experiences there, a confirmation as reliable as that provided by your neighbors in England about your experiences there) or it could remain private ("in this case everyone would inhabit two real spaces, one common to all and one peculiar to each" [143]).

But, Quinton anticipates the objection, the lake place is *not real*—no one, in fact, can locate it. So? "Why," asks Quinton, "do we have this ontological wastepaper basket for the imaginary?" (144). Is it because, he wonders, there are no consequences in our imaginary world and we thus don't have to take it seriously? But there *are* consequences in the lake world and you *do* take it seriously (you fall on your fish spear, remember?). Interpreted this way, Quinton says, reality doesn't need to be located in a (single) physical space.

Can the same be said about time? Can we conceive two coherent experiences such that the people *within* each experience are temporally related but there is no temporal relation *between* the two experiences? This doesn't seem possible, Quinton says: "If an experience is mine it is memorable, and if it is memorable it is temporally connected to my present state" (146); in other words, unless you remember the experiences of the one world while in the other, there's no reason to say you are in both worlds, but if you do remember the experiences of the one while in the other, then the worlds aren't in two separate times. So, Quinton concludes, while our concepts of experience need not be spatial (see "Strawson's No-Space World" for agreement on this point), it does need to be temporal (see "Shoemaker's Time-Freezing World" for disagreement on this point).

SHOEMAKER'S TIME-FREEZING WORLD

Consider . . . the following world. To the best of the knowledge of the inhabitants of this world, all of its matter is contained in three relatively small regions, which I shall call A, B, and C. These regions are separated by natural boundaries, but it is possible, usually, for the inhabitants of this world to pass back and forth from one region to another, and it is possible for much of what occurs in any of the regions to be seen by observers situated in the other regions. Periodically there is observed to occur in this world a phenomenon which I shall call a "local freeze." During a local freeze all processes occurring in one of the three regions come to a complete halt; there is no motion, no growth, no decay, and so on. At least this is how it appears to observers in the other regions. During a local freeze, it is impossible for people from other regions to pass into the region where the freeze exists, but when inhabitants of other regions enter it immediately following the end of a freeze, they find that everything is as it would have been if the period of the freeze had not occurred. . . . Those people who were in the region during the freeze will initially be completely unaware that the period of the freeze has elapsed, unless at the beginning of the freeze they happened to be observing one of the other regions. . . . To such a person it will appear as if all sorts of major changes have occurred instantaneously in the other region. . . .

. . . [L]et us suppose that it is found that in region A local freezes have occurred every third year, that in region B local freezes have occurred every fourth year, and that in region C local freezes have occurred every fifth year. Having noticed this they could easily calculate that . . . there should be simultaneous local freezes . . . in all three regions every sixtieth year. Since these three regions exhaust their universe, to say that there will be simultaneous local freezes in all three regions every sixtieth year is to

Source: Sydney Shoemaker. "Time Without Change." *Journal of Philosophy* 66.12 (1969): 363–381. 369–370, 370–371. Copyright © 1969 Journal of Philosophy, Inc. Reprinted by permission of the publisher and author.

say that every sixtieth year there will be a *total* freeze lasting one year. Let us suppose . . . that no freeze is observed to begin by anyone at the time at which local freezes are scheduled to begin simultaneously in all three regions, and that the subsequent pattern of freezes is found to be in accord with the original generalization about the frequency of freezes. If all of this happened, I submit, the inhabitants of this world would have grounds for believing that there are intervals during which no changes occur anywhere.

———

The purpose of Shoemaker's thought experiment is to establish that, contrary to the widely held view that the passage of time necessarily involves change, it is conceptually possible for there to be time without change. But would the inhabitants of this world have grounds for believing that to be so, as Shoemaker claims?

One objection, anticipated by Shoemaker, focuses on the generalization to a simultaneous freeze in all three areas every sixtieth year: the inhabitants could have as easily generalized to predict that freezes occur every third, fourth, and fifth year, in areas A, B, and C, respectively, *with the exception* that all three regions skip a freeze every 59 years. According to this generalization, since there would never be a freeze in all three areas at the same time, there would never be a time without change. Why should the inhabitants accept the generalization they did instead of this alternate one? Shoemaker's answer appeals to the principle of simplicity (often called Occam's Razor): when there are equally reasonable competing explanations, accept the one that's simpler. But why?

Another, and perhaps more intriguing, objection to his thought experiment is that it doesn't provide a way for the total freeze to come to an end. Presumably, in the case of local freezes, some preceding event in an adjacent nonfrozen area causes the unfreezing of the frozen area, but in the case of a total freeze (that is, a time *without change*), what would cause the change from frozen to unfrozen? Can the mere passage of time have causal force?

And so, if, as Shoemaker's experiment shows, it *is* possible for there to be time without there being change, how can we know that *we* haven't undergone a total freeze, lasting perhaps billions of years, between "yesterday" and "today"?

Locke's Voluntary Prisoner

[S]uppose a man be carried, whilst fast asleep, into a room where is a person he longs to see and speak with; and be there locked fast in, beyond his power to get out: he awakes, and is glad to find himself in so desirable company, which he stays willingly in, i.e. prefers his stay to going away. I ask, is not this stay voluntary?

Source: John Locke. *An Essay Concerning Human Understanding.* Book 2, Chapter 21, Section 10. 1690. As collated and annotated by Alexander Campbell Fraser. New York: Dover, 1959. Volume 1. 317.

It is perhaps easy to think that voluntary action is evidence of freedom. This thought experiment shows otherwise. Locke claims that the man's staying in the room *is* voluntary (he stays willingly), but it is *not free:* "So far as a man has power to think or not to think, to move or not to move, according to the preference or direction of his own mind, so far is a man *free*" (315). Choosing to do something makes the action voluntary, but unless you could actually do otherwise (the man can't leave), the action is not free. (But since we can do only one thing, we can never really know whether we really *could* have done otherwise. Right?)

Locke claims, therefore, that questions about "free will" don't make sense—"freedom" and "will" are two different things: will is the capacity to think of various actions and choose whichever is preferable, whereas freedom is the capacity to actually do as one wills. So the question isn't whether *the will* is free, says Locke, but whether *a person* is free.

Which should bear on moral responsibility—the voluntariness or the freedom? Is it that a person is morally responsible for doing X as long as she does X because she *chooses* to do X—*whether or not* she could have done otherwise? Or is it that a person is morally responsible for doing X only if he could have done otherwise (in which case determinism is incompatible with moral responsibility—in a determined world, we can't do other than what we do, so we can't be held morally responsible for our actions)?

JAMES'S WAY HOME

What is meant by saying that my choice of which way to walk home after the lecture is ambiguous and matter of chance as far as the present moment is concerned? It means that both Divinity Avenue and Oxford Street are called; but that only one, and that one *either* one, shall be chosen. Now, I ask you seriously to suppose that this ambiguity of my choice is real; and then to make the impossible hypothesis that the choice is made twice over, and each time falls on a different street. In other words, imagine that I first walk through Divinity Avenue, and then imagine that the powers governing the universe annihilate ten minutes of time with all that it contained, and set me back at the door of this hall just as I was before the choice was made. Imagine then that, everything else being the same, I now make a different choice and traverse Oxford Street. You, as passive spectators, look on and see the two alternative universes—one of them with me walking through Divinity Avenue in it, the other with the same me walking through Oxford Street. Now, if you are determinists, you believe one of these universes to have been from eternity impossible: you believe it to have been impossible because of the intrinsic irrationality or accidentality somewhere involved in it. But looking outwardly at these universes, can you say which is the impossible and accidental one, and which the rational and necessary one?

Source: William James. "The Dilemma of Determinism." 1884. As reprinted in William James, *The Will to Believe and Other Essays in Popular Philosophy.* Cambridge, MA: Harvard University Press, 1979. 114–140. 121.

James's answer to the question he poses at the end of his thought experiment is "no": "In other words, either universe *after the fact* and once there would, to our means of observation and understanding, appear just as rational as the other" (121); any of the many possible futures would extend rationally from our past and present. Thus James hopes to have shown that our disturbance at indeterminism (according to which the universe is not "fixed"—one event does not necessarily determine others), stemming as it does from the ambiguity or chance regarding the future that threatens to turn our world into "a sort of insane sand-heap" (121), is hollow. But *does* his scenario show that such ambiguity or chance need not entail irrationality? And is that all there is to our "fear" of indeterminism?

Further, James says that from a strictly theoretical point of view, the question of whether the world is determined or not is insoluble; however, from a practical point of view, it makes sense to assume indeterminism and to act as if one has freedom of will—because without freedom of will, our actions would be neither good nor bad.

LYON'S CARD PREDICTOR

[S]uppose that a man A, holding six black cards and one red card in his hand, says to man B, "I am now going to lay the cards one at a time face upwards on the table in front of me. . . ."

. . .

. . . Suppose that B . . . [says] that he [can] predict which card A [is] going to lay first. A might say, ridiculously enough, "Well, which card *am* I going to lay first?", and when B says "Black," A always lays red, and *vice versa*. . . .

Does this scenario prove we have free will?

Source: Ardon Lyon. "The Prediction Paradox." *Mind* 68.272 (1959): 510–517. 512, 515.

Lyon believes the scenario, imaginary but perfectly plausible, *does* prove that we have free will. But does it prove that A has free will, or does it just prove that B was wrong in his prediction? For if B's prediction is not just a guess, but is based on knowledge of a determined future, a future in which only one action (the predicted one) is possible, it is hard to see that A *can* act otherwise and choose to lay down the other card.

Instead of arguing that free will is impossible (given determinism), one might argue that determinism is impossible (given free will)—because of the effect of the prediction on the predictee. The reasoning would go something like this: If I say "black," you'll lay the red card just to spite me; so I'll say "red," you'll lay a black card, and I'll be right. But you won't be right if you said "red"—or rather, you'll be right only if what you *say* you're predicting isn't what you're *really* predicting. If we make sincerity a condition, the problem remains. But the problem that remains is with prediction, not determinism, right? (What exactly is the relation between the two?)

GOLDMAN'S BOOK OF LIFE

While browsing through the library one day, I noticed an old dusty tome, quite large, entitled "Alvin I. Goldman." I take it from the shelf and start reading. In great detail, it describes my life as a little boy. It always gibes with my memory and sometimes even revives my memory of forgotten events. I realize that this purports to be a book of my life, and I resolve to test it. Turning to the section with today's date on it, I find the following entry for 2:36 P.M. "He discovers me on the shelf. He takes me down and starts reading me. . . ." I look at the clock and see that it is 3:03. It is quite plausible, I say to myself, that I found the book about half an hour ago. I turn now to the entry for 3:03. It reads: "He is reading me. He is reading me. He is reading me." I continue looking at the book in this place, meanwhile thinking how remarkable the book is. The entry reads: "He continues to look at me, meanwhile thinking how remarkable I am."

I decide to defeat the book by looking at a future entry. I turn to an entry 18 minutes hence. It says: "He is reading this sentence." Aha, I say to myself, all I need do is refrain from reading that sentence 18 minutes from now. I check the clock. To ensure that I won't read that sentence, I close the book. My mind wanders; the book has revived a buried memory and I reminisce about it. I decide to reread the book there and relive the experience. That's safe, I tell myself, because it is an earlier part of the book. I read that passage and become lost in reverie and rekindled emotion. Time passes. Suddenly I start. Oh yes, I intended to refute the book. But what was the time of the listed action?, I ask myself. It was 3:19, wasn't it? But it's 3:21 now, which means I have already refuted the book. Let me check and make sure. I inspect the book at the entry for 3:17. Hmm, that seems to be the wrong place for there it says I'm in a reverie. I

Source: Alvin I. Goldman. "Actions, Predictions, and Books of Life." *American Philosophical Quarterly* 5.3 (1968): 135–151. 143–144.

skip a couple of pages and suddenly my eyes alight on the sentence: "He is reading this sentence." But it's an entry for 3:21, I notice! So I made a mistake. The action I had intended to refute was to occur at 3:21, not 3:19. I look at the clock, and it is still 3:21. I have not refuted the book after all.

Would Goldman ever be able to falsify the predictions made in his "book of life"? If not, does that prove the world, and our lives, are determined?

Goldman continues his thought experiment a little further, describing two more predicted events that he considers falsifying, but he finds that he has good reasons (currently existing reasons in the one case, new and unanticipated reasons in the other case) to do as predicted, and so he does. It would seem, then, that his answer to the first question is "no"—in the world he has constructed, which is a determined world, he will not be able to falsify the predictions. As for the second question, Goldman's intent is not to show that our lives are determined, but rather that determinism is *compatible* with our lives as we experience them—that is, as having voluntary behavior such as deliberation, choice, and decision.

But so what? Do we want to know our choices are *compatible* with the real world, or do we want to know they have *causal* force (rather than being merely ineffectual illusions)? Goldman seems to suggest the latter is the case (as well as the former), claiming that although our action is determined, or causally necessitated, "one of the antecedent conditions which necessitate it is [our] deliberation" (150). Still, doesn't something seem "wrong" about "deliberating" over a decision that's inevitable?

FRANKFURT'S WILLING ADDICT

Suppose . . . a willing addict, who would not have things any other way. If the grip of his addiction should somehow weaken, he would do whatever he could to reinstate it; if his desire for the drug should begin to fade, he would take steps to renew its intensity.

Does the addict have free will?

Source: Harry G. Frankfurt. "Freedom of the Will and the Concept of a Person." *Journal of Philosophy* 68.1 (1971): 5–20. 19.

If "having free will" means one can choose to do otherwise, then no, the addict does not have free will; because of his addiction, he cannot choose to do otherwise.

However, Frankfurt provides an alternative account of free will. He suggests that while many creatures have first-order desires (desires to do this or that), it is the presence of additional, second-order desires (desires *about* desires to do this or that, desires that indicate reflective self-evaluation) that separates "persons" from other creatures. When our will is in accord with those second-order desires, when those desires move us to act in accord with them, then, says Frankfurt, we have free will. One can act freely (do what one wants) and still not have a free will. Consider a dog with no second-order desires who is able to satisfy all her first-order desires—for example, to run whenever and wherever she wants. And one can be *unable* to act freely and still *have* a free will. Consider someone *unaware* that she is unable to do X—she may still quite freely will to do X. Just as free action means one is free to *do* what one wants, free will means one is free to *will* what one wants; when you have the will you want to have—when your will conforms to your second-order desires—you have free will. So, Frankfurt says, because the addict is acting according to his second-order desires (he wants to be an addict—he wants to want the drug), he does have a free will. Even though his will is in fact beyond his control, it is nevertheless in accord with his desires.

Is it though? How can we be sure his desires (first order or second order) aren't likewise beyond his control because of the addiction? (See "Taylor's Ingenious Physiologist.")

Taylor's Ingenious Physiologist

[W]e can suppose that an ingenious physiologist can induce in me any volition he pleases, simply by pushing various buttons on an instrument to which, let us suppose, I am attached by numerous wires. All the volitions I have in that situation are, accordingly, precisely the ones he gives me. By pushing one button, he evokes in me the volition to raise my hand; and my hand, being unimpeded, rises in response to that volition. By pushing another, he induces the volition in me to kick, and my foot, being unimpeded, kicks in response to that volition. We can even suppose that the physiologist puts a rifle in my hands, aims it at some passer-by, and then, by pushing the proper button, evokes in me the volition to squeeze my finger against the trigger, whereupon the passer-by falls dead of a bullet wound.

Am I free?

Source: Richard Taylor. *Metaphysics.* 2nd edition. Englewood Cliffs, NJ: Prentice-Hall, 1974. 50.

If everything in the universe is determined, it would seem that we can't have free will. (Though it may be important to define determinism—for example, to say that everything is determined, or caused, by preexisting conditions is not necessarily to say that at any given time only one action is possible.) "Compatibilism" (a view claiming that free will is compatible with determinism) provides a "solution" to this "problem" by defining freedom as the absence of obstacles that prevent one from doing something and/or forces that compel one to do something. Thus, one can be free (free of obstacles and forces) even in a causally determined world—free to act according to one's volitions or desires.

Taylor's thought experiment is intended to challenge compatibilism: one may be free to act according to one's desires (that is, one is neither prevented nor compelled), but as long as one's desires are caused by something (as indeed they must be, according to determinism), then one is hardly free. But, one might respond, that "something" may be our own selves (and not some ingenious physiologist): *we* are responsible for our desires because of past choices (that make us who and what we are) and/or because of our reasoning about our options. What if you had *asked* the physiologist to "cause" those desires? Consider a person who hires a hypnotist to implant the desire to go outside. Is he not acting according to free will? (When he hires the hypnotist *and* when he later goes outside?) And yet, what makes us choose as we do in the past? What makes us reason as we do? Can't who and what we are (including the capacity to change who and what we are) be attributed solely to our genetic makeup and the events that happened to us—both of which are external causes, as "compelling" as the ingenious physiologist? Consider Gardner's turtles: "[Imagine] a mechanical turtle that crawls across the floor in obedience to internal mechanisms. It moves here and there, seemingly at random. Contrast this with a toy turtle that a child pulls with a string. The toy is compelled by outside forces to move as it does, whereas the mechanical turtle is under no extraneous compulsion" (Martin Gardner, *The Whys of a Philosophical Scrivener,* 105). Is either one free?

Note that if the world is *not* determined, we also can't have free will, for in a world in which events are not caused, our will would have no effect at all on our actions.

But does it have to be "all or nothing"? Can't we say that some events are caused and some not? But then, which are which? Perhaps events are caused by a constellation of preexisting conditions, and perhaps in the case of human behavior, our will is one of them. So is it that our will *influences* but does not completely cause our behavior?

GAUNILO'S LOST ISLAND

$[I]$t is said that somewhere in the ocean is an island, which . . . is called the lost island. And they say that this island has an inestimable wealth of all manner of riches and delicacies in greater abundance than is told of the Islands of the Blest; and that having no owner or inhabitant, it is more excellent than all other countries, which are inhabited by mankind, in the abundance with which it is stored.

Now if some one should tell me that there is such an island, I should easily understand his words, in which there is no difficulty. But suppose that he went on to say, as if by a logical inference: "You can no longer doubt that this island which is more excellent than all lands exists somewhere, since you have no doubt that it is in your understanding. And since it is more excellent not to be in the understanding alone, but to exist both in the understanding and in reality, for this reason it must exist. For if it does not exist, any land which really exists will be more excellent than it; and so the island already understood by you to be more excellent will not be more excellent."

Should I believe him?

Source: Gaunilo. "In Behalf of the Fool." c. 1078. As rendered in *Anselm's Basic Writings.* 2nd edition. S. N. Deane, trans. Chicago: Open Court Publishing, 1962. As reprinted in *The Ontological Argument: From St. Anselm to Contemporary Philosophers.* Alvin Plantinga, ed. Garden City, NY: Anchor Books, 1965. 7–13. 11.

The ontological argument for the existence of a supreme god, attributed first to Anselm (*Proslogion,* 1078), is as follows: we can conceive of God, something that is greater in all ways than anything else; a something that actually exists in reality is greater than a something that exists only in our mind; therefore, God actually exists. In short, God is "that than which a greater cannot be conceived." Unlike the argument from design (see "Paley's Watch"), which appeals to the perceived facts of experience (an *a posteriori* argument), Anselm's argument appeals solely to the concepts of reason (an *a priori* argument).

Gaunilo wrote a critique of Anselm's proof of God's existence, of which the "Lost Island" is a part. "If," Gaunilo says, "a man should try to prove to me by such reasoning that this island truly exists, . . . I should believe that he was jesting" (11). One might think Gaunilo's objection is simply that one can't bring something into existence merely by imagining it: we can imagine the most beautiful island, but that doesn't mean it has to exist. However, there is more to the objection than that, because Anselm isn't saying simply that God is most *beautiful*—he's saying God is most *everything.* And being the most everything has to include existing. But, Gaunilo says, it *doesn't* have to: excellence doesn't necessarily imply existence. Indeed, why should it? What's so great about existing that an X that exists is greater than an X that doesn't exist? Is it (always) better to exist than not to exist?

One might also challenge the circularity that seems to be present in Anselm's argument: if you define God as something that exists (and Anselm does this by saying that "greatest conceivable" includes "exist"), then hasn't he assumed before he started what he set out to prove?

In one of his replies to Gaunilo, Anselm says, further, that "by no means can this being than which a greater cannot be conceived be understood as any other than that which alone is greater than all" (21). He thus "ensures" the Christian notion of a *single* god. But why is the quality of uniqueness, as well as existence, entailed? "That than which nothing greater can be conceived" is slightly, but significantly, different from "greater than all things" (a phrase Anselm seems to use interchangeably with the other one); two (or more) things can be *equally* great *and* such that nothing greater than them could be conceived—can't they?

Pascal's Wager

If there is a God, He is infinitely incomprehensible, since, having neither parts nor limits, He has no relation to us. . . .

Who then will blame Christians for inability to give a reason for their belief, professing as they do a religion for which they can give no reason? . . . Let us then examine this point and say "God is or is not." But which way shall we lean? Reason can settle nothing here; there is an infinite gulf between us [Christians and atheists]. A game is on, at the other end of this infinite distance, and heads or tails will turn up. What will you wager? According to reason you cannot do either; according to reason you cannot leave either undone.

. . .

. . . Since you must choose, let us see what concerns you least. You have two things to lose: truth and good, and two things to stake: your reason and your will, your knowledge and your happiness. And your nature has two things to shun: error and misery. Your reason does not suffer by your choosing one more than the other, for you must choose. That is one point cleared. But your happiness? Let us weigh gain and loss in calling heads that God is. Reckon these two chances: if you win, you win all; if you lose, you lose naught.

Source: Blaise Pascal. *Pensées.* no. 223. 1670. H. F. Stewart, trans. New York: Pantheon Books, 1965. 117, 119.

Pascal urges us, "Do not hesitate, wager that He is" (no. 223), and asks pointedly, "What have you to lose?" (no. 223).

Well, one might respond, if it turns out your belief that "God is" is incorrect, you will have lost the earthly pleasures you may have chosen to forego because of that belief; you win all (eternal bliss in Heaven) only if your belief turns out to be correct. But that's rather Pascal's point: what's the loss of a few earthly pleasures against the possibility of eternal bliss? Too, if you wager "God is not" and you're wrong, you stand to lose even more, as you'd face eternal suffering in Hell.

But, one might also respond, Pascal's wager will succeed in convincing us that belief in a Christian god is reasonable (which was Pascal's purpose—he didn't intend his wager to provide any proof of that god's existence) only if we also or already believe in the Christian system of reward and punishment. *Is* there a Heaven? *Is* it a place of eternal bliss? And *is* it reserved for those who believe in a certain god? (As comic Jass Richards quips, "What if there *is* a God, and Heaven is only for those bright enough to recognize there's no *proof* that he exists?")

HUME'S INFANT, INFERIOR, OR SUPERANNUATED DEITY

[Suppose that a person with a very limited intelligence] were brought into the world [and assured] that it was the workmanship of . . . a sublime and benevolent Being; he might, perhaps, be surprised [at finding it so full of vice and misery and disorder]; but would never retract his former belief, if founded on any very solid argument; since such a limited intelligence must be sensible of his own blindness and ignorance, and must allow that there may be many solutions of those phenomena which will forever escape his comprehension. But suppos[e] . . . that this creature is not antecedently convinced of a supreme intelligence, benevolent, and powerful, but is left to gather such a belief from the appearance of things.

Will he find reason to conclude the world was the work of such a powerful, wise, and benevolent deity?

Source: David Hume. *Dialogues Concerning Natural Religion.* Part XI. 1779. As reprinted in *The English Philosophers from Bacon to Mill.* Edwin A. Burtt, ed. New York: Random House, 1967. 690–764. 745.

H ume's answer is "no"—if we consider the world without the bias of previous belief, he claims, we would *not* conclude that it was created by such a deity. He thus does not accept the argument from design (see "Paley's Watch").

In fact, Hume suggests, given the "contrivance or economy of the animal creation, by which pains, as well as pleasures, are employed to excite all creatures to action" (746), "the conducting of the world by general laws" (747), "the frugality with which all powers and faculties are distributed to every particular being" (748), and "the inaccurate workmanship of all the springs and principles of the great machine of nature" (749)—all of which give rise to the miseries of natural evil—it may be far more reasonable to conclude that the world is "the first rude essay of some infant deity, who afterwards abandoned it, ashamed of his lame performance" (720), or "the work . . . of some dependent, inferior deity and . . . the object of derision to his superiors" (720), or "the production of old age and dotage in some superannuated deity and ever since his death, has run on" (720). (Is it?)

PALEY'S WATCH

In crossing a heath, suppose I pitched my foot against a *stone,* and were asked how the stone came to be there; I might possibly answer that for anything I knew to the contrary, it had lain there forever; nor would it perhaps be very easy to show the absurdity of this answer. But suppose I had found a *watch* upon the ground, and it should be inquired how the watch happened to be in that place.

Source: William Paley. *Natural Theology, or Evidences of the Existence and Attributes of the Deity Collected from the Appearances of Nature.* 1802. As reprinted in *A Modern Introduction to Philosophy: Readings from Classical and Contemporary Sources.* 3rd edition. Paul Edwards and Arthur Pap, eds. New York: The Free Press, 1973. 419–434. 419.

Paley's response is that "the watch must have had a maker" (420) because "its several parts are framed and put together for a purpose [that being to tell time]" (419). He then reasons that since the natural world shows not only as much but more design toward a purpose, it too must have had a maker. This "argument from design" for the existence of a creator god is actually, then, an argument by analogy: the watch is to the watchmaker as the natural world is to the creator god.

But is the analogy sound? First, *is* the natural world as "framed and put together" as a watch? One can point to several instances that suggest not. Paley would respond that he needs only one instance of design—and he focuses on the human eye—in order to conclude that there is indeed a designer. One might then point out that the human eye isn't very well designed; for example, it's useless unless there's light. But, Paley would respond, imperfections in design are relevant to the *attributes* of a creator (such imperfections might suggest, for example, an unimaginative or inept designer); he is establishing only the *existence* of a creator.

Second, *do* the parts of the natural world work together "for some purpose"? One might respond that the purpose of much of the natural world, ourselves included, is not as evident as the purpose of the watch. Paley might respond that it doesn't matter whether we understand how the parts work together—it matters only that they are designed to do so. But if we don't know what the purpose of the natural world is, how can we say it *is* designed for some purpose?

Even if the parts of the natural world do fit together, achieving some purpose, is a creator god the only explanation possible? Perhaps the world is that way by chance. Paley would say the watch—and by analogy, the natural world—is too complicated, too organized, to have been the result of chance—a pimple might be the result of chance, but not an eye! (*Is* a stone so different from a watch?)

Perhaps the world was always that way. Paley would say that appealing to some infinite regress still leaves design unaccounted for.

Or perhaps, as evolutionary theory suggests, the parts fit together because those that didn't fit together (didn't adapt to their environment) didn't survive. The evolutionary theory does seem to challenge Paley's argument, but it need not challenge his conclusion: advocates of theistic evolution would argue that a god designed the developmental processes that led to the world we have (rather than, as Paley claims, designing the world as is).

Wisdom's Long-Neglected Garden

Two people return to their long neglected garden and find among the weeds a few of the old plants surprisingly vigorous. One says to the other, "It must be that a gardener has been coming and doing something about these plants." Upon inquiry they find that no neighbor has ever seen anyone at work in their garden. The first man says to the other, "He must have worked while people slept." The other says, "No, someone would have heard him and besides, anybody who cared about the plants would have kept down these weeds." The first man says, "Look at the way these are arranged. There is purpose and a feeling for beauty here. I believe that someone comes, someone invisible to mortal eyes. I believe that the more carefully we look the more we shall find confirmation of this." They examine the garden ever so carefully and sometimes they come on new things suggesting that a gardener comes and sometimes they come on new things suggesting the contrary and even that a malicious person has been at work. Besides examining the garden carefully, they also study what happens to gardens left without attention. Each learns all the other learns about this and about the garden. Consequently, when after all this, one says, "I still believe a gardener comes," while the other says, "I don't," their different words now reflect no difference as to what they have found in the garden, no difference as to what they would find in the garden if they looked further and no difference about how fast untended gardens fall into disorder. . . . What is the difference between them?

Source: John Wisdom. "Gods." *Proceedings of the Aristotelian Society* 45 (1944–1945): 185–206. 191–192.

Wisdom engages in this thought experiment in order to examine "the logic of belief in divine minds" (187). A belief is reasonable, he says, if there are facts that support it, but the two people who have returned to their garden agree on what the facts of the matter are. So how is it that one believes there is a gardener and the other doesn't? Perhaps their difference in opinion is due not to the facts per se but to the perceived support provided by those facts. And disputes about whether certain facts are indeed sufficient to support certain conclusions may be settled, Wisdom says, by tracing the elements of the argument and their connections to each other, by identifying fallacious reasoning ("mis-connections"), and by exposing hidden assumptions. When this is done to the arguments of the two people in the scenario, what will be the result?

Antony Flew has rewritten Wisdom's scenario (in "Theology and Falsification"), describing test after test conducted by the believer in order to establish the gardener's existence. As each test fails, the believer qualifies his claim, and this eventually leads the skeptic to ask, no doubt with some frustration, "Just how does what you call an invisible, intangible, eternally elusive gardener differ from an imaginary gardener or even from no gardener at all?"

Hick's Resurrected People

First picture: Suppose that at some learned gathering in this country, one of the company were suddenly and inexplicably to disappear, and that at the same moment, an exact replica of him were suddenly and inexplicably to appear at some comparable meeting in Australia. The person who appears in Australia is exactly similar, as to both bodily and mental characteristics, with the person who disappears in America. There is continuity of memory, complete similarity of bodily features, including even fingerprints, hair and eye coloration, and stomach contents, and also of beliefs, habits, and mental propensities. In fact there is everything that would lead us to identify the one who appeared with the one who disappeared, except continuity of occupancy of space. . . .

Second picture: Now let us suppose that the event in America is not a sudden and inexplicable disappearance, and indeed not a disappearance at all, but a sudden death. Only, at the moment when the individual dies, a replica of him as he was at the moment before his death, complete with memory up to that instant, appears in Australia. . . .

Third picture: My third supposal is that the replica, complete with memory, etc. appears, not in Australia, but as a resurrection replica in a different world altogether, a resurrection world inhabited by resurrected persons. This world occupies its own space, distinct from the space with which we are now familiar. . . .

Can we not imagine this?

Source: John Hick. "Theology and Verification." *Theology Today* 17.1 (1960): 12–31. 22, 23.

This thought experiment is presented in the context of a discussion about whether or not the existence of the Christian god is, in principle, verifiable. That is to say, can we at least *imagine* some experience that would prove that such a god exists? "Life after death"—that is, "continued conscious existence after bodily death" (16)—is such an experience, claims Hick. However, others claim that such a concept of immortality is unintelligible: the self cannot exist without the physical body. Hick's thought experiment is designed to show that the idea of life after death *is* intelligible, that we *can* imagine, without contradiction, continued conscious existence after bodily death. (And so the existence of the Christian god is thus, in principle, verifiable).

But, one might ask, considering the third picture, how will the person know he has really died? Maybe he just fell asleep and then woke up—so it's not life after death after all. Hick adds to his picture the possibility that the person will meet in the resurrection world people he knows to have died.

Even with that addition, does Hick's experiment demonstrate what he thinks it demonstrates? Perhaps immortality *is* intelligible, and perhaps such immortality is in accord with the concept of the Christian god. But is it in accord *only* with a Christian god? Perhaps life after death verifies some other god or just that death as we know it isn't the end many of us think it is. To this, Hick merely adds another possibility to his picture, the possibility that the person will in some way meet with the Christian god in the resurrection world.

But how will the person *know* that he has met with that god—how can a mere human *recognize* a transcendent being with qualities that so exceed human experience? Hick's reply is that the Christian god reveals himself to us through Jesus Christ, so if the person were to meet Jesus Christ in the resurrection world, that would suffice to verify the Christian god's existence (though, as Hick concedes, that existence would be verified only for that person). Is that too big an "if"?

And is verification *in principle* of any significant value?

Hick's World with Flexible Laws of Nature

Suppose, contrary to fact, that this world were a paradise from which all possibility of pain and suffering were excluded. The consequences would be very far-reaching. . . . [N]o one would ever be injured by accident: the mountain-climber, steeplejack, or playing child falling from a height would float unharmed to the ground; the reckless driver would never meet with disaster. . . . [T]here would be no call to be concerned for others in time of need or danger, for in such a world there could be no real needs or dangers.

To make possible this continual series of individual adjustments, nature would have to work by "special providences" instead of running according to general laws which men must learn to respect on penalty of pain or death. The laws of nature would have to be extremely flexible: sometimes gravity would operate, sometimes not; sometimes an object would be hard and solid, sometimes soft. There could be no sciences, for there would be no enduring world structure to investigate.

Would such a world be the best of all possible worlds?

Source: John Hick. *Philosophy of Religion.* Englewood Cliffs, NJ: Prentice-Hall, 1963. 44–45.

Hick's world with flexible laws of nature is part of a response to arguments against the loving and all-good god of Judeo-Christian religions that point to the fact of evil as negating the existence of such a god. Hick deals with "moral evil"—the pain and suffering caused by people's actions—by saying that "only persons [that is, only beings with free will] could, in any meaningful sense, become 'children of God,' capable of entering into a personal relationship with their Creator by a free and uncompelled response to his love" (43). This thought experiment is intended to address "non-moral evil" or "natural evil"—the pain and suffering caused by natural phenomena such as earthquakes, droughts, and so on.

According to Hick, God created the world as "a place of 'soul-making' in which free beings, grappling with the tasks and challenges of their existence in a common environment, may become 'children of God' and 'heirs of eternal life'" (44), and this growth could not occur in a world without real dangers and the possibility of real pain. "Courage and fortitude would have no point in an environment in which there is, by definition, no danger or difficulty," Hick says; "[g]enerosity, kindness, the *agape* aspect of love, prudence, unselfishness, and all other ethical notions which presuppose life in a stable environment, could not even be formed" (45). In short, in a world without natural laws, and the consequent pain and suffering, we couldn't develop moral qualities, and we couldn't therefore become "children of God"—the world he has imagined would be "the worst of all possible worlds" (45).

But what evidence do we have for Hick's claim that some god created the world as a "soul-making" place? And isn't Hick making a circular argument—assuming an all-good god to show that the fact of evil doesn't disprove the existence of an all-good god? And what about sentient animals (presumably without souls) that suffer horrible pain as a result of forest fires and other natural events (see "Rowe's Fawn")—is it right (or inevitable) that we become "children of God" at their expense?

And does a world without pain and suffering necessarily mean a world without consistent laws of nature? Can't we imagine a world with consistent laws of nature, in which instead of pain we feel just a tingling sensation (when we fall or collide or whatever)? (Or, if that's not "motivating" enough, consider Hume's suggestion that there be no pain, but only varying levels of pleasure; one would withdraw one's hand from the fire in order to avoid the sudden drop in pleasure.)

Plantinga's Curley Smith and Transworld Depravity

[S]uppose that] Curley Smith, the mayor of Boston, is opposed to the proposed freeway route. From the Highway Department's point of view, his objection is frivolous; he complains that the route would require destruction of the Old North Church along with some other antiquated and structurally unsound buildings. The Director of Highways offers him a bribe of $35,000 to drop his opposition. Unwilling to break with the fine old traditions of Bay State politics, Curley accepts. . . .

. . .

. . . [Suppose further that] Curley's bribability is utter and absolute. . . .
. . . [N]o matter *what* circumstances [God] places Curley in, so long as he leaves him significantly free, he will take at least one wrong action. . . .
. . . Curley suffers from what I shall call *transworld depravity.*

Is it not possible therefore that God cannot create a world without moral evil?

Source: Alvin Plantinga. *The Nature of Necessity.* London: Oxford University Press, 1974. 173–174, 185, 186.

Plantinga's Curley Smith will do at least one wrong thing in all possible worlds, and it is possible, Plantinga suggests, that everyone is like Curley Smith—that we *all* suffer from transworld depravity. Therefore, he concludes, it may be that God can*not* create a world in which people are free but in which they do no wrong. Plantinga thus provides with this thought experiment a response to those who say that if God were truly all-powerful and all-good, he would have created a world in which people have free will but nevertheless do no wrong. (And, thus, Plantinga upholds the "free will defense" against the existence of evil, the defense that moral evil is an inevitable by-product of our free will.)

But, one might respond, couldn't God have created people *without* transworld depravity? Or at least without depravity in just *one* world (preferably ours)? If so, though, one must then ask whether people who *always* do right *are* free. Well, if we are free and *sometimes* do right, is it not logically possible to be free and *always* do right? How does freedom *depend* on actually doing wrong?

ROWE'S FAWN

Suppose in some distant forest lightning strikes a dead tree, resulting in a forest fire. In the fire a fawn is trapped, horribly burned, and lies in terrible agony for several days before death relieves its suffering. So far as we can see, the fawn's intense suffering is pointless. For there does not appear to be any greater good such that the prevention of the fawn's suffering would require either the loss of that good or the occurrence of an evil equally bad or worse. Nor does there seem to be any equally bad or worse evil so connected to the fawn's suffering that it would have had to occur had the fawn's suffering been prevented. . . . Since the fawn's intense suffering was preventable and, so far as we can see, pointless, doesn't it appear that . . . there do exist instances of intense suffering which an omnipotent, omniscient being could have prevented without thereby losing some greater good or permitting some evil equally bad or worse?

Source: William L. Rowe. "The Problem of Evil and Some Varieties of Atheism." *American Philosophical Quarterly* 16.4 (1979): 335–341. 337.

R owe anticipates we will respond in the affirmative, and thus accept the first premise of an argument for atheism: "There exist instances of intense suffering which an omnipotent, omniscient being could have prevented without thereby losing some greater good or permitting some evil equally bad or worse" (336). The second premise, "An omniscient, wholly good being would prevent the occurrence of any intense suffering it could, unless it could not do so without thereby losing some greater good or permitting some evil equally bad or worse" (336), leads, then, to the conclusion, "There does not exist an omnipotent, omniscient, wholly good being" (336).

However, Rowe anticipates an objection: "Perhaps, for all we know, there is some familiar good outweighing the fawn's suffering to which that suffering is connected in a way we do not see. Furthermore, there may well be unfamiliar goods, goods we haven't dreamed of, to which the fawn's suffering is inextricably connected" (337)—so we can't *know* that the first premise is true. But, he responds, we do have *rational grounds* for believing it to be true. Is that sufficient?

Even if, Rowe continues, it should somehow be reasonable to believe the fawn's suffering is inextricably connected to some greater good or to some equally bad or worse evil (though appeals to character development can't be made, since surely any character development expected of the fawn is not encouraged by being burnt to death, and appeals to free will can't be made, since the fire was caused by lightning), it's unlikely that's true of *all* the instances of intense suffering that occur daily. (So it wouldn't change anything if Rowe's fawn were a particularly bad little fawn? And a bunch of other little fawns saw from a distance its horrible death?)

LOCKE'S INVERTED SPECTRUM

[Suppose] by the different structure of our organs it were so ordered, that *the same object should produce in several men's minds different ideas* at the same time; for example, if the idea that a violet produced in one man's mind by his eyes were the same that a marigold produced in another man's and vice versa.

———————

Could this be known to be so?

Source: John Locke. *An Essay Concerning Human Understanding.* Book 2, Chapter 32, Section 15. 1690. As collated and annotated by Alexander Campbell Fraser. New York: Dover, 1959. Volume 1. 520.

Locke's response is that we could not know if this were so "because one man's mind could not pass into another man's body, to perceive what appearances were produced by those organs" (520). The possibility that another person's experience of the same thing may be different from your own (for example, that his or her color spectrum may be inverted relative to yours), and the impossibility of knowing this, underscores the absolute subjectivity of experience: we can experience only "the view from here" (see "Nagel's Bat"). One of the implications of this is the limitation it puts on establishing truth: there is simply no way to prove or disprove subjective experiences.

Another implication is that if we can't know the contents of other minds, can we even know there *are* other minds? (This is called the "other minds" problem. See "Kirk and Squires's Zombies.")

Contemporary developments of this thought experiment postulate not an *inter*subjective difference, but an *intra*subjective one: suppose that a person's own spectrum has changed—as a result of inverting glasses, neurological rewiring, or transport to a planet with yellow skies and red grass. Such suppositions are intended to challenge the view that mental states are equivalent to functional states or behaviors. That such a person may long for the way the colors used to be shows that her mental state has changed (for example, she now experiences something different when she sees red) even though her functional state has not (for example, after a period of adaptation, she can still stop when she sees a "red" light)—thus, one can conclude, there are two independent states involved. Or not—if her actual subjective experience reverted (and it wasn't just that she had adapted to the inverted subjective experience), then mental states may be equivalent to functional states after all.

LEIBNIZ'S MACHINE

Suppose that there be a machine, the structure of which produces thinking, feeling, and perceiving; imagine this machine enlarged but preserving the same proportions, so that you could enter it as if it were a mill. This being supposed, you might visit its inside; but what would you observe there? Nothing but parts which push and move each other, and never anything that could explain perception.

Source: Gottfried Wilhelm von Leibniz. *Monadology.* Section 17. 1714. Paul Schrecher and Anne Martin Schrecher, trans. Indianapolis: Bobbs-Merrill, 1965. 150.

The point of Leibniz's thought experiment is that thinking, feeling, and perceiving cannot be explained by mechanism, by mere parts and movements of parts (as claimed by materialists). In other words, there is more to the mind than the brain (as claimed by dualists). What "more" could this be? Leibniz's explanation involves a sort of harmonious orchestration by God of simple elements (monads) that bond together and form composites (matter).

But we know today that mental states have measurable correlates—electrical and biochemical changes—in the brain. And indeed, if the mind were truly something separate from the brain, why would brain injuries affect mental features like reason, emotion, and consciousness? So perhaps there *isn't* more to the mind than the brain.

And yet a brain scan can indicate only *that* we're thinking, not *what* we're thinking. Furthermore, the actual *experience* of thinking is not at all like the corresponding brain state. Has Leibniz missed the importance of point of view? Does his thought experiment just prove that thinking, feeling, and perceiving are not *visible* processes—that is, visible from a third-person perspective? (How could they be "visible" from a first-person perspective?)

A criticism of Leibniz's thought experiment is that it assumes the whole is no more than the sum of its parts. David Cole (in "Thought and Thought Experiments") has designed a counter–thought experiment to illustrate this fallacy of composition: "Imagine a drop of water expanded in size until each molecule is the size of a grindstone in a mill. If you walked through such a now mill-sized drop of water, you might see wondrous things but you would see nothing *wet*. But this hardly shows that water does not consist *solely* of H_2O molecules." That is, water need not consist of something additional to H_2O molecules to account for its wetness, just as Leibniz's machine, the brain, need not consist of something additional to its neurons and so on to account for thoughts, feelings, and perceptions. (True?)

TURING'S IMITATION GAME

[T]he "imitation game" . . . is played with three people, a man (A), a woman (B), and an interrogator (C) who may be of either sex. The interrogator stays in a room apart from the other two. The object of the game for the interrogator is to determine which of the other two is the man and which is the woman. . . . The interrogator is allowed to put questions to A and B. . . .

In order that tones of voice may not help the interrogator, the answers should be written, or better still, typewritten. The ideal arrangement is to have a teleprinter communicating between the two rooms. . . .

We now ask the question, "What will happen when a machine takes the part of A in this game?" Will the interrogator decide wrongly as often when the game is played like this [between a machine and a human being] as he does when the game is played between a man and a woman? These questions replace our original, "Can machines think?"

Source: A. M. Turing. "Computing Machinery and Intelligence." *Mind* 59.236 (1950): 433–460. 433–434.

The question "Will the interrogator be able to tell which is the machine and which the human being?" is an empirical one—and one that is actually answered every year at the annual Turing Test Competition, in which people enter their computer programs as competitors alongside human competitors. Apparently interrogators are *not* able to tell: computers *have* been mistaken for human beings by panels of very expert judges. (And, perhaps as interesting, human beings have been mistaken for computers.) What questions would one ask to determine which was the human and which the computer?

And would one thereby determine whether machines can *think?* How do we define "think"? (And how do we define "machine"?) Has Turing set the bar too low? That is, could something pass his test and still not be able to think? (See "Searle's Chinese Room.") Is it a mistake to infer internal processes from external behavior? Or has he set it too high? (What are we to say of those human beings who failed the test?)

"Instead of trying to produce a programme to simulate the adult mind," Turing suggests, "why not rather try to produce one which simulates the child's?" (456)—perhaps we should be trying to program machines not to think, but to learn. (Is *that* the definition of "think" we're looking for?)

Yet another question arises: so what? Are we establishing the ability to think as a criterion for personhood (see "Warren's Space Traveler") and thus for certain rights and responsibilities? (Which ones?) Is that a good criterion to use? A necessary one (that is, you *have* to be able to think to be granted those rights and responsibilities)? A sufficient one (that is, being able to think is *all* you have to be able to do)?

KIRK AND SQUIRES'S ZOMBIES

Imagine an exact physical replica of a given man—something we may conveniently dub a "Zombie replica." Would such an exact physical replica be an exact replica of that man?

Source: Robert Kirk and J. E. R. Squires. "Zombies v. Materialists." *Aristotelian Society* supplementary vol. 48 (1974): 135–163. This is a composite statement from pages 135 and 141.

Philosophers have used the idea of zombies, perhaps first articulated by Kirk and Squires, to investigate the materialist view that human beings are *not* more than physical objects. (See "Leibniz's Machine.") The materialist would say "yes, the zombie is an exact replica" (in which case, we couldn't tell who's a zombie and who's not). (Or more correctly—in which case, we'd all be zombies.)

The dualist would say "no, even though an exact *physical* replica, the zombie's missing something." A soul? A mind? (So having a brain, that physical stuff in our skulls, is not enough?) (What if consciousness—for which, many suggest, we need a mind—is nothing more than the presence of certain physical stuff?) (So the zombie would be conscious. . . .)

NAGEL'S BAT

I assume we all believe that bats have experience. After all, they are mammals, and there is no more doubt that they have experience than that mice or pigeons or whales have experience. . . .

. . . Now we know that most bats (the microchiroptera, to be precise) perceive the external world primarily by sonar, or echolocation, detecting the reflections, from objects within range, of their own rapid, subtly modulated, high-frequency shrieks. Their brains are designed to correlate the outgoing impulses with the subsequent echoes, and the information thus acquired enables bats to make precise discriminations of distance, size, shape, motion, and texture comparable to those we make by vision. . . .

. . . [But] I want to know what it is like for a *bat* to be a bat.

Source: Thomas Nagel. "What Is It like to Be a Bat?" *Philosophical Review* 83.4 (1974): 435–450. 438, 439.

Can we say? Can we know what it's like to be a bat? Nagel's response is that we can't say—we can't know what it's like *for a bat* to *be* a bat: "[B]at sonar, though clearly a form of perception, is not similar in its operation to any sense that we possess, and there is no reason to suppose that it is subjectively like anything we can experience or imagine. This appears to create difficulties for the notion of what it is like to be a bat" (438). We might be able to say what it would be like for *us* to be a bat, but not what it is like *for the bat* to be a bat. "Even if I could by gradual degrees be transformed into a bat," says Nagel, "nothing in my present constitution enables me to imagine what the experiences of such a future stage of myself thus metamorphosed would be like" (439). In fact, Nagel suggests, while this would most certainly be true as well of any extraterrestrial life form we may meet, it is also true of other human beings—we may not even be able to say what it's like for another person to be that person (unless he or she is sufficiently similar to ourselves).

Nagel is investigating here the relation between mind and body, which is, he says, particularly difficult because of consciousness: "[T]he fact that an organism has conscious experience *at all* means, basically, that there is something it is like to *be* that organism" (436)—he calls that something the subjective character of experience. "What it's like" is accessible only from one point of view, the viewpoint of the subject (see "Locke's Inverted Spectrum"). Therefore, since the subjective experience can't be accessed by anyone outside the subject, inferences from observable physical behavior (body) to mental states (mind) seem questionable. One might wonder, then, since we can't know the nature of others' experiences, can we at least know they have them? Can we at least know there's a "they"—that there *are* other minds?

Is Nagel correct? Can we never imagine something that is totally *outside,* totally *beyond,* our own experience? (Can we describe the taste of chocolate to someone who has never tasted it?)

BLOCK'S CHINESE NATION

Imagine a body externally like a human body, say yours, but internally quite different. The neurons from sensory organs are connected to a bank of lights in a hollow cavity in the head. A set of buttons connects to the motor-output neurons. Inside the cavity resides a group of little men. Each has a very simple task: to implement a "square" of a reasonably adequate machine table that describes you. On one wall is a bulletin board on which is posted a state card, i.e., a card that bears a symbol designating one of the states specified in the machine table. Here is what the little men do: Suppose the posted card has a "G" on it. This alerts the little men who implement G squares—"G-men" they call themselves. Suppose the light representing input I_{17} goes on. One of the G-men has the following as his sole task: when the card reads "G" and the I_{17} light goes on, he presses output button O_{191} and changes the state card to "M." This G-man is called upon to exercise his task only rarely. In spite of the low level of intelligence required of each little man, the system as a whole manages to simulate you because the functional organization they have been trained to realize is yours. . . .

. . .

Suppose we convert the government of China to functionalism, and we convince its officials that it would enormously enhance their international prestige to realize a human mind for an hour. We provide each of the billion people in China (I chose China because it has a billion inhabitants) with a specially designed two-way radio that connects them in the appropriate way to other persons and to the artificial body mentioned in the previous example. We replace the little men with a radio transmitter and receiver connected to the input and output neurons. Instead of a bul-

Source: Ned Block. "Troubles with Functionalism." *Minnesota Studies in the Philosophy of Science* 9 (1978): 261–325. 278–280.

letin board, we arrange to have letters displayed on a series of satellites placed so that they can be seen from anywhere in China. Surely such a system is not physically impossible. It could be functionally equivalent to you for a short time, say an hour.

Does this system have mental states?

Those who claim that mental states can be explained by the nonmental states of function or organization would say the Chinese nation *does* have mental states; since it is functionally equivalent to you, it would have the mental states you have. Block disagrees, however: the Chinese nation would *not* have mental states, because neurologically and psychologically it is unlike you (and you have mental states). So do mental states (minds) depend on neurology (brains)? What exactly is meant here by "depend"?

One may agree with Block intuitively, because it is hard to imagine the Chinese nation so described as being conscious, but surely it is equally hard to imagine the brain being conscious.

Perhaps the Chinese nation *does* have mental states—they're just not like the mental states we have. But how could we know this?

And would whatever conclusion that is reached be true for both nonqualitative mental states (for example, thoughts, desires, intentions) as well as qualitative mental states (for example, the way pain feels and the way red seems)? That is, do the different kinds of mental states have different relationships to either physical/material states or functional/organizational states?

Rorty's Antipodeans

F_{ar} away, on the other side of our galaxy, there was a planet on which lived beings like ourselves—featherless bipeds who built houses and bombs, and wrote poems and computer programs. These beings did not know that they had minds. They had notions like "wanting to" and "intending to" and "believing that" and "feeling terrible" and "feeling marvelous." But they had no notion that these signified *mental* states—states of a peculiar and distinct sort—quite different from "sitting down," "having a cold," and "being sexually aroused." . . . [T]hey did not explain the difference between persons and non-persons by such notions as "mind," "consciousness," "spirit," or anything of the sort. . . .

In most respects, then, the language, life, technology, and philosophy of this race were much like ours. But there was one important difference. Neurology and biochemistry had been the first disciplines in which technological breakthroughs had been achieved, and a large part of the conversation of these people concerned the state of their nerves. When their infants veered toward hot stoves, mothers cried out, "He'll stimulate his C-fibers!" . . . Their knowledge of physiology was such that each well-formed sentence in the language which anybody bothered to form could easily be correlated with a readily identifiable neural state.

What can we say about the Antipodeans with respect to mental phenomena?

Source: Richard Rorty. *Philosophy and the Mirror of Nature.* Princeton, NJ: Princeton University Press, 1979. 70–71.

Rorty hopes to show with his Antipodeans that we can do quite well without conceptualizing a "mind"; our notion of "mental" and "physical" is a mistaken inheritance from the seventeenth century. Reference to neural states could sufficiently replace all our talk about mental states. This is not to deny the existence of things like pain, for what the Antipodeans report when they say "Stimulated C-fibers!" is what we report when we say "Pain!" Nor is this to deny that "pain" "hurts"—the Antipodeans avoid stimulated C-fibers just as we avoid pain.

One might question, however, whether reference to neural states could cover not only mental states such as pain but also mental states such as thoughts, beliefs, intentions, desires, and so on. Rorty seems to suggest it could when he says the following of his Antipodeans (71–72):

> Sometimes they would say things like "It looked like an elephant, but then it struck me that elephants don't occur on this continent, so I realized that it must be a mastodon." But they would also sometimes say, in just the same circumstances, things like "I had G-412 together with F-11, but then I had S-147, so I realized that it must be a mastodon."

Could knowledge of physiology be such that every sentence we wanted to form could be correlated with a neural state?

SEARLE'S CHINESE ROOM

Consider a language you don't understand. In my case, I do not understand Chinese. To me Chinese writing looks like so many meaningless squiggles. Now suppose I am placed in a room containing baskets full of Chinese symbols. Suppose also that I am given a rule book in English for matching Chinese symbols with other Chinese symbols. The rules identify the symbols entirely by their shapes and do not require that I understand any of them. The rules might say such things as, "Take a squiggle-squiggle sign from basket number one and put it next to a squoggle-squoggle sign from basket number two."

Imagine that people outside the room who understand Chinese hand in small bunches of symbols and that in response I manipulate the symbols according to the rule book and hand back more small bunches of symbols. Now, the rule book is the "computer program." The people who wrote it are "programmers," and I am the "computer." The baskets full of symbols are the "data base," the small bunches that are handed in to me are "questions" and the bunches I then hand out are "answers."

Now suppose that the rule book is written in such a way that my "answers" to the "questions" are indistinguishable from those of a native Chinese speaker. For example, the people outside might hand me some symbols that unknown to me mean, "What's your favorite color?" and I might after going through the rules give back symbols that, also unknown to me, mean, "My favorite is blue, but I also like green a lot." I satisfy the Turing test for understanding Chinese. All the same, I am totally ignorant of Chinese. And there is no way I could come to understand Chinese in

Source: John R. Searle. "Is the Brain's Mind a Computer Program?" *Scientific American* 262 (1990): 26–31. 26. First presented in "Minds, Brains, and Programs." *Behavioral and Brain Sciences* 3 (1980): 417–424.

the system as described, since there is no way that I can learn the meanings of any of the symbols. Like a computer, I manipulate symbols, but I attach no meaning to the symbols.

Does this not refute the view that computers think?

———

As an analogue for computers, Searle's Chinese Room is intended to refute the view that computers think. "If I do not understand Chinese solely on the basis of running a computer program for understanding Chinese," Searle says, "then neither does any other digital computer solely on that basis" (26). More to the point, "a program merely manipulates symbols, whereas a brain attaches meaning to them" (26). (See "Turing's Imitation Game.")

One objection to Searle's experiment is that the person could not possibly put out such correct replies *without* understanding Chinese. No program, no set of rules, could possibly enable him to do so (see "Quine's Gavagai"). But computers do just that (put out correct replies to questions put in)—don't they?

Another objection is that while the person in the room doesn't understand Chinese, the whole room does; the person is like a single neuron in the brain that by itself doesn't understand but contributes to the understanding of the whole system. But, Searle replies, how could it? Simply shuffling the symbols around doesn't give access to the meanings of the symbols—to the person *or* to the room.

One might wonder, however, whether the person in the room wouldn't eventually come to understand Chinese. (But how? By paying attention to correspondences between the questions it receives and the answers it assembles? What is it, what is required, to "pay attention"?) Likewise, a computer program might *develop* understanding, might come to know the meanings of the symbols and rules it uses. But how could that occur? Would the computer program itself be sufficient for that? If not, what else might it need? A certain size or speed or complexity? An additional metaprogram? A certain "biological" or "organic" component? (A brain? To cause a mind?)

Putnam's Brain in a Vat

$[I]$magine that a human being (you can imagine this to be yourself) has been subjected to an operation by an evil scientist. The person's brain (your brain) has been removed from the body and placed in a vat of nutrients which keeps the brain alive. The nerve endings have been connected to a super-scientific computer which causes the person whose brain it is to have the illusion that everything is perfectly normal. There seem to be people, objects, the sky, etc., but really all the person (you) is experiencing is the result of electronic impulses travelling from the computer to the nerve endings. The computer is so clever that if the person tries to raise his hand, the feedback from the computer will cause him to "see" and "feel" the hand being raised. Moreover, by varying the program, the evil scientist can cause the victim to "experience" (or hallucinate) any situation or environment the evil scientist wishes. He can also obliterate the memory of the brain operation, so that the victim will seem to himself to have always been in this environment. It can even seem to the victim that he is sitting and reading these very words about the amusing but quite absurd supposition that there is an evil scientist who removes people's brains from their bodies and places them in a vat of nutrients which keep the brains alive.

Could we be brains in a vat?

Source: Hilary Putnam. *Reason, Truth, and History.* Cambridge, UK: Cambridge University Press, 1981. 5–6.

Though the possibility of being a brain in a vat is often used to make an epistemological point (see "Descartes's Evil Demon"), Putnam uses it to explore the relationship between the mind and the external world. Though the brain in the vat may be conscious and intelligent, the words it thinks do not—cannot—refer to what our words refer to; the words of the brain in the vat necessarily refer to the images generated by the vat machinery, not to the actual external objects we call, for example, trees. But the images generated by the vat machinery are similar, indeed identical, to, say, trees—so how can we say the brain isn't therefore referring to real trees? Consider, responds Putnam, an ant whose path turns out to have traced a perfect image of Winston Churchill: surely we won't say the ant has drawn a picture of Winston Churchill—similarity is not enough for us to say that something represents something else.

"So," continues Putnam, "if we really are brains in a vat, then the sentence 'We are brains in a vat' says something false (if it says anything)" (15)—for the words would not be referring to real things. The supposition that we are brains in a vat is, thus, self-refuting (one whose truth implies its own falsity—see "The Liar Paradox"): "In short, if we are brains in a vat, then 'We are brains in a vat' is false" (15). (So we can't possibly be brains in a vat.)

Putnam's larger point is about the preconditions of reference and hence thought: "[O]ne cannot refer to certain kinds of things, e.g., *trees,* if one has no causal interaction at all with them, or with things in terms of which they can be described" (16–17). But can't we refer to unicorns? Yes, but we have causal interaction with horses and two-horned goats. Okay, doesn't what happens to the brain in the vat—the back-and-forth experience of neural signals—count as "causal interaction"? (So maybe we *are* brains in a vat. . . .)

JACKSON'S MARY, THE BRILLIANT COLOR SCIENTIST

Mary is a brilliant scientist who is, for whatever reason, forced to investigate the world from a black and white room *via* a black and white television monitor. She specializes in the neurophysiology of vision and acquires, let us suppose, all the physical information there is to obtain about what goes on when we see ripe tomatoes, or the sky, and use terms like "red," "blue," and so on. She discovers, for example, just which wavelength combinations from the sky stimulate the retina, and exactly how this produces *via* the central nervous system the contraction of the vocal chords and expulsion of air from the lungs that results in the uttering of the sentence "The sky is blue." . . .

What will happen when Mary is released from her black and white room or is given a color television monitor? Will she *learn* anything or not?

Source: Frank Jackson. "Epiphenomenal Qualia." *Philosophical Quarterly* 32 (1982): 127–136. 130.

Jackson goes on to say that Mary *will* learn something—which means, then, that her previous knowledge was incomplete, that she was "missing something." And since her previous knowledge consisted of physical information, that means that physicalism—the view that all mental experiences can be explained by physical material or processes—should be rejected as incomplete. Jackson says, "There are certain features of the bodily sensations especially, but also of certain perceptual experiences, which no amount of purely physical information includes" (127).

In a similar thought experiment, Jackson postulates Fred, someone who can see a color we can't (not just a different shade or hue of a color we *can* see, but a whole new color). Jackson argues that although we may know all the physical stuff about Fred (we know all about his unique optical system, for example—and everything about the rest of his body, for that matter), we will still not know what that color is like, what it's like to see that color. (See "Molyneux's Blind Man" and "Nagel's Bat".)

But Mary does have vision, and she does see black and white. Wouldn't she be able to extrapolate from that knowledge and all her information to knowledge of red, blue, and so on? One might think so, but consider that our knowledge of red, blue, and so on doesn't seem sufficient for us to then know what color Fred sees. And yet, if Mary does indeed have "all the physical information there is to obtain about what goes on when we see ripe tomatoes"—what more is there to know? (What exactly might she learn? Are there different kinds of knowledge?)

Maybe Mary *can* see red but her experience of seeing red is different from our experience of seeing red. . . . (See "Locke's Inverted Spectrum.")

SEARLE'S BRAIN REPLACEMENT

Imagine that [as your brain gradually deteriorates, it becomes] entirely replaced by silicon chips. . . . In such a situation there would be various possibilities. One logical possibility . . . [is that] you continue to have all of the sorts of thoughts, experiences, memories, etc., that you had previously; the sequence of your mental life remains unaffected. In this case, we are imagining that the silicon chips have the power not only to duplicate your input-output functions, but also to duplicate the mental phenomena, conscious and otherwise, that are normally responsible for your input-output functions.

. . .

. . . A second possibility . . . [is that] as the silicon is progressively implanted into your dwindling brain, you find that the area of your conscious experience is shrinking, but that this shows no effect on your external behavior. You find, to your total amazement, that you are indeed losing control of your external behavior. You find, for example, that when the doctors test your vision, you hear them say, "We are holding up a red object in front of you; please tell us what you see." You want to cry out, "I can't see anything. I'm going totally blind." But you hear your voice saying in a way that is completely out of your control, "I see a red object in front of me." If we carry this thought experiment out to the limit, we get a much more depressing result than last time. We imagine that your conscious experience slowly shrinks to nothing, while your externally observable behavior remains the same.

. . .

Now consider a third variation. In this case, we imagine that the progressive implantation of the silicon chips produces no change in your mental life, but you are progressively more and more unable to put your

Source: John Searle. *The Rediscovery of the Mind.* Cambridge, MA: MIT Press, 1992. 66–68. Originally appeared in *Scientific American,* January 1990. Copyright 1989 by Scientific American, Inc. All rights reserved. Reprinted by permission.

thoughts, feelings, and intentions into action. In this case, we imagine that your thoughts, feelings, experiences, memories, etc., remain intact but your observable external behavior slowly reduces to total paralysis. . . . So in this case, you might hear the doctors saying, "The silicon chips are able to maintain heartbeat, respiration, and other vital processes, but the patient is obviously brain dead. We might as well unplug the system. . . ." Now in this case, you would know that they are totally mistaken. That is, you want to shout out, "No, I'm still conscious! I perceive everything going on around me. It's just that I can't make any physical movement. I've become totally paralyzed."

───────────

Searle explores with this extended thought experiment the possible causal relationship between consciousness, behavior, and the brain. He hopes to show that "the capacity of the brain to cause consciousness is conceptually distinct from its capacity to cause motor behavior. A system could have consciousness without behavior and behavior without consciousness" (69).

But can we really imagine the second possibility? How would the brain know what behavior to cause? Can we answer that question without reference to any mental processes? We can imagine it for certain behavior, such as reflex movements, but can we imagine it for the vision test Searle describes? If not, is our failure to do so just a failure of imagination—in which case Searle's point may still stand?

In an interesting and related thought experiment, David Chalmers ("Absent Qualia, Fading Qualia, Dancing Qualia") argues that the second possibility is not, in fact, possible. If we were to gradually replace one's neurons with silicon chips, he asks, would one's consciousness gradually fade (as Searle suggests) or suddenly blink out? The latter would mean that consciousness depended on a single neuron (when that one was replaced, the "lights went out" so to speak)—which is unlikely. However, the former is also unlikely, because if you were to continue reporting red objects (as Searle suggests), that would mean you were out of touch with your conscious experience—which is also unlikely. Chalmers concludes, then, that the qualia (the quality or feel of conscious sensory experience) would stay the same during the replacement. And if the functional organization remains the same (no matter what the physical stuff actually is), the consciousness will remain the same (see "Block's Chinese Nation").

HOBBES'S SHIP OF THESEUS

$\begin{bmatrix} I \end{bmatrix}$f . . . that ship of Theseus [were continually repaired by] taking out the old planks and putting in new . . . and if some man had kept the old planks as they were taken out, and by putting them afterwards together in the same order, had again made a ship of them, [which ship would be the original one?]

Source: Thomas Hobbes. *De Corpore,* Part 2, Chapter 11, "Of Identity and Difference." 1655. As reprinted in Thomas Hobbes. *Body, Man, and Citizen,* Richard S. Peters, ed. New York: Collier Books, 1962. 128.

R eferred to as early as 75 CE by Plutarch, the ship of Theseus, with its planks being continually replaced, has long been a focal point for discussions about identity. Hobbes adds the possibility of building a ship out of the old planks, asking the general question, "What is it to be the same?" or, conversely, "What is it to be different?" He considers three possible answers. First, one could determine identity (that is, one could identify the thing *as* the thing) by the *matter* of the thing—a lump of wax is the same lump of wax whether it's spherical or cubical, and so the reconstructed ship is the original one. (What if the planks were used to build a house—would the house be the ship?) However, according to this view, because a person's body (matter) changes over time, a person who is punished for a crime committed some time ago isn't actually the same person who committed the crime—which suggests an injustice. (See "Parfit's Nobelist.") (Does it matter how quickly the person's body changes? How continuously? How completely?)

Second, one could determine identity by the *form* of the thing—even though a person's body has changed, it is still a singular body occupying a single place in space. However, according to this view, the repaired ship Hobbes describes would be the original ship—but so would the reconstructed ship. This is, Hobbes says, absurd—some one thing can't be in two places at the same time. (What if the ship is not repaired as the old planks are removed, and some time elapses before it is reconstructed—where is the ship in that meantime?)

Third, one could determine identity by the aggregate of qualities or attributes (magnitude, motion, power, and so on) the thing has. But according to this view, nothing would be the same as it was—neither ship would be the original one, and furthermore, someone sitting down would become a different person as soon as she stood up.

So what is it to be the same, or different? How shall we determine identity? Hobbes's answer is that we pay careful attention to what exactly it is we're inquiring about: "It is one thing to ask concerning Socrates, whether he be the same man, and another to ask whether he be the same body" (128). So, Hobbes concludes, "a ship, which signifies matter so figured, will be the same as long as the matter remains the same; but if no part of the matter be the same, then it is numerically another ship; and if part of the matter remain and part be changed, then the ship will be partly the same, and partly not the same" (129); furthermore, "a man will be always the same, whose actions and thoughts proceed all from the same beginning of motion, namely, that which was in his generation" (129). But isn't it a body, a *changing* body, that provides that "*same* beginning of motion"?

Locke's Prince and Cobbler

For should the soul of a prince, carrying with it the consciousness of the prince's past life, enter and inform the body of a cobbler, as soon as deserted by his own soul, every one sees he would be the same *person* with the prince, accountable only for the prince's actions: but who would say it was the same *man?*

Source: John Locke. *An Essay Concerning Human Understanding.* Book 2, Chapter 27, Section 15. 1690. As collated and annotated by Alexander Campbell Fraser. New York: Dover, 1959. Volume 1. 457.

With this thought experiment, Locke suggests that "persons" are independent of "bodies" and what makes a person a person, and the *same* person, is consciousness—awareness of one's thoughts and actions: "Nothing but consciousness can unite remote existences into the same person" (464). Referring to a man he'd met who believed his soul had been the soul of Socrates, Locke asks, "If the man truly were Socrates in a previous life, why doesn't he remember any of Socrates' thoughts or actions?" (See "Leibniz's King of China" and "Reid's Brave Officer.") Locke even says that if your little finger is cut off and consciousness should happen to go along with the finger, leaving the rest of the body, then that little finger would be the person—the same person that was, just before, identified with the whole body (459–460).

Locke also says that after the soul change, the now "prince-cobbler" (having the cobbler's body) "would be the same cobbler to every one besides himself" (457). How would the "prince-cobbler" know he's still the prince? How do we know, when we wake up each morning after a period of unconsciousness, that we are still ourselves? Because we remember what we did yesterday? But we remember what other people did yesterday, too. Because we remember what we thought and felt yesterday? Is there something special about the memories we have of our *selves,* something special about *self*-consciousness?

REID'S BRAVE OFFICER

Suppose a brave officer to have been flogged when a boy at school, for robbing an orchard, to have taken a standard [a flag] from the enemy in his first campaign, and to have been made a general in advanced life: suppose also, which must be admitted to be possible, that, when he took the standard, he was conscious of his having been flogged at school, and that when made a general he was conscious of his taking the standard, but had absolutely lost the consciousness of his flogging.

Is the general the same person as the boy?

Source: Thomas Reid. *Essays on the Intellectual Powers of Man.* 1785. As edited by A. D. Woozley. London: Macmillan, 1941. 213.

This thought experiment is intended to illustrate a weakness in Locke's theory that personal identity depends on our consciousness or memory of our thoughts and actions and can be extended backwards only as far as that consciousness or memory goes. If that were so, Reid says, then the officer is the same person as the boy, and the general is the same person as the officer, but the general is *not* the same person as the boy. And yet logic indicates that the general *is* the same person as the boy (if A = B and B = C, then A = C). Reid therefore rejects Locke's view (and accepts the logic). But is the logic applicable in this case? Does "=" mean the same as "is the same person as"?

Reid suggests, instead, that the succession from A to B to C is sufficient for identity: "My thoughts, and actions, and feelings change every moment—they have no continued, but a successive existence; but that *self* of *I* to which they belong is permanent, and has the same relation to all the succeeding thoughts, actions, and feelings, which I call mine" (203). (See "Parfit's Teletransporter.") Perhaps, then, part of the problem is just our sloppy way of talking—do we really mean that the officer *is* the same person as the boy or that the officer is the person the boy has *become?*

Reid points out further problems with Locke's view: it confounds consciousness with memory (are they the same?), and it confounds personal identity with evidence of personal identity (can't you have the one without the other?). Memory is *evidence that* I am who I was, says Reid; it is not what *makes* me who I was (remembering that you did something doesn't make you to have done it).

Pointing to our ever changing consciousness, Reid also asks, in further critique of Locke's view, "Is it not strange that the sameness or identity of a person should consist in a thing which is continually changing and is not any two minutes the same?" (214).

Lastly, Reid says, if our personal identity consists in consciousness, then "as our consciousness sometimes ceases to exist, as in sound sleep, our personal identity must cease with it. Mr. Locke allows that the same thing cannot have two beginnings of existence; so . . . our identity would be irrecoverably gone every time we cease to think, if it was but for a moment" (216). And that is, Reid implies, absurd.

So if it's neither consciousness nor memory, what is it that makes you the same person tomorrow—or ten years from tomorrow—as you are today? (Or are you someone else every time you wake up?) (And do you have a problem with that?)

LEIBNIZ'S KING OF CHINA

Let us suppose that some individual suddenly became King of China, but only on condition that he forgot what he had been, as if he had just been reborn: does that not come to the same in practice, or in the effects that could be registered, as if he had to be annihilated and a King of China created at the same instant and at the same place?

Source: Gottfried Wilhelm von Leibniz. *Discourse on Metaphysics,* Section 34. 1846. R. Niall, D. Martin, and Stuart Brown, trans. Manchester, UK: Manchester University Press, 1988. 80.

Leibniz is suggesting, along with Locke (see "Locke's Prince and Cobbler"), that what makes us who we are is our memories—if the individual he describes were to have lost his memories, he may as well have been annihilated. What is it that our memories provide for identity—uniqueness? richness? continuity? And which memories are important in this regard—facts? skills? experiences?

Further, how much of one's memory is required to retain one's identity? If we are required to be conscious of or remember *all* of our thoughts and actions, then none of us is the same person we once were. (See "Parfit's Teletransporter.") Is one more of oneself the more one remembers of one's life? What are the implications of this view for people who experience injuries or illnesses that deprive them of their memories? What about mistaken memories regarding past experiences? What about fading memories—would that indicate a fading self? What are the implications for all of us who lose, simply as time passes, first the sharpness of our memories and then the memories themselves?

Lastly, is memory the *only* element required for our identity?

WILLIAMS'S CHARLES AND GUY FAWKES— AND ROBERT

Suppose [a] man who underwent [a] radical change of character—let us call him Charles—claimed, when he woke up, to remember witnessing certain events and doing certain actions which earlier he did not claim to remember; and that under questioning he could not remember witnessing other events and doing other actions which earlier he did remember. . . .

. . .

. . . [Suppose that] all the events he claims to have witnessed and all the actions he claims to have done point unanimously to the life-history of some one person in the past—for instance, Guy Fawkes. Not only do all Charles' memory-claims that can be checked fit the pattern of Fawkes' life as known to historians, but others that cannot be checked are plausible, provide explanations of unexplained facts, and so on. Are we to say that Charles is now Guy Fawkes, that Guy Fawkes has come to life again in Charles' body, or some such thing?

Source: Bernard Williams. "Personal Identity and Individuation." *Proceedings of the Aristotelian Society* 57 (1957): 229–252. 233, 237–238.

Williams says "no" and thus argues, against Locke and others (see "Locke's Prince and Cobbler"), that bodily identity is a necessary (though not sufficient) condition of personal identity. One of Williams's points is that while it is logically impossible that two different people remember being the same person who did certain things, it is not logically impossible that two different people *claim* to remember being that same person—and we cannot in fact establish anything more than the claim (for how could we possibly determine that Charles and Guy Fawkes actually do have the same first-person memories?). (But how does what we can or cannot establish bear on what can or cannot be?)

Further, Williams says, "if it is logically possible that Charles should undergo the changes described, then it is logically possible that some other man should simultaneously undergo the same changes; e.g., that both Charles and his brother Robert should be found in this condition. What should we say in that case? They cannot both be Guy Fawkes; if they were, Guy Fawkes would be in two places at once, which is absurd" (238). So the best we can say in this case, Williams suggests, is that both Charles and Robert had become *like* Guy Fawkes—and if that's the best description in the second case, when there are two (Charles and Robert), why wouldn't it also be the best description in the first case, when there is just one (Charles)?

One of the problems, however, with using the body as a criterion for identity, especially if one says that that's a *sufficient* criterion (which Williams does *not*) is that our bodies last longer than "we" do. (How exactly is that a problem?)

SHOEMAKER'S BROWNSON

So let us imagine the following. . . . One day, to begin our story, a surgeon discovers that an assistant has made a horrible mistake. Two men, a Mr. Brown and a Mr. Robinson, had been operated on for brain tumors, and brain extractions had been performed on both of them. At the end of the operations, however, the assistant inadvertently put Brown's brain in Robinson's head, and Robinson's brain in Brown's head. One of these men immediately dies, but the other, the one with Robinson's body and Brown's brain, eventually regains consciousness. Let us call the latter "Brownson." Upon regaining consciousness, Brownson exhibits great shock and surprise at the appearance of his body. Then, upon seeing Brown's body, he exclaims incredulously, "That's me lying there!" Pointing to himself, he says, "This isn't my body; the one over there is!" When asked his name he automatically replies, "Brown." He recognizes Brown's wife and family (whom Robinson had never met), and is able to describe in detail events in Brown's life, always describing them as events in his own life. Of Robinson's past life, he evidences no knowledge at all. Over a period of time, he is observed to display all of the personality traits, mannerisms, interests, likes and dislikes, and so on that had previously characterized Brown, and to act and talk in ways completely alien to the old Robinson.

What would we say if such a thing happened?

Source: Sydney Shoemaker. *Self-Knowledge and Self-Identity.* Ithaca, NY: Cornell University Press, 1963. 23–24.

Since, Shoemaker claims, we would say that Brownson is actually Brown in Robinson's body, we are not using the body as our criterion for identity. (Note the use of "in"—indeed note that we say "I *have* a body" rather than "I *am* a body"—which suggests that one's self is somehow separate from one's body.) (Or maybe we're just speaking wrongly. Perhaps the whole notion of "I" is an unfortunate and mistaken by-product of our language.) (Can you imagine a language without "I"? Can you imagine the people who would have such a language?)

But the brain is part of the body, one might respond. To this, Shoemaker points out that we're not really using the brain as our criterion either: "If upon regaining consciousness, Brownson were to act and talk just as Robinson had always done in the past" (24), then we'd say it's Robinson even though he has Brown's brain. So we're actually using psychological features—personality and memory of past events. And since we think such psychological features are causally related to the brain, we figure Brownson will have the personality features and memories of Brown rather than of Robinson.

But does the rest of one's body have *no* causal relationship to one's psychological features? Not even developmentally? That is, if one's body happens to be robust, might one not develop more confidence than if one's body happened to be otherwise? And so might not Brown with Robinson's body become, sooner or later, a different person than he was when he had his own body? (How long would Brownson remain Brown if Brown had been white skinned and Robinson had been black skinned, or if Brown had been female and Robinson had been male?)

WILLIAMS'S BODY EXCHANGE/MIND SWAP

Suppose that there were some process to which two persons, A and B, could be subjected as a result of which they might be said—question-beggingly—to have *exchanged bodies*. That is to say—less question-beggingly—there is a certain human body which is such that when previously we were confronted with it, we were confronted with person A, certain utterances coming from it were expressive of memories of the past experiences of A, certain movements of it partly constituted the actions of A and were taken as expressive of the character of A, and so forth; but now, after the process is completed, utterances coming from this body are expressive of what seem to be just those memories which previously we identified as memories of the past experiences of B, its movements partly constitute actions expressive of the character of B, and so forth; and conversely with the other body.

. . .

. . . We further announce that one of the two resultant persons, the A-body-person and the B-body-person, is going after the experiment to be given $100,000 while the other is going to be tortured. We then ask each A and B to choose which treatment should be dealt out to which of the persons who will emerge from the experiment, the choice to be made (if it can be) on selfish grounds.

. . .

Let us now consider something apparently different. Someone in whose power I am tells me that I am going to be tortured tomorrow. I am frightened, and look forward to tomorrow in great apprehension. He adds that when the time comes, I shall not remember being told that this was going to happen to me, since shortly before the torture something else will be done to me which will make me forget the announcement.

Source: Bernard Williams. "The Self and the Future." *Philosophical Review* 79.2 (1970): 161–180. 161, 163, 167–168. Copyright © 1970 Cornell University.

This certainly will not cheer me up. . . . He then adds that my forgetting the announcement will be only part of a larger process: when the moment of torture comes, I shall not remember any of the things I am now in a position to remember. This does not cheer me up, either. . . . He now further adds that at the moment of torture I shall not only not remember the things I am now in a position to remember, but will have a different set of impressions of my past, quite different from the memories I now have. I do not think that this would cheer me up, either. . . . Nor do I see why I should be put into any better frame of mind by the person in charge adding lastly that the impressions of my past with which I shall be equipped on the eve of torture will exactly fit the past of another person now living, and that indeed I shall acquire these impressions by (for instance) information now in his brain being copied into mine. . . .

Williams suggests that in the first case, A would probably choose that the B-body person should get the $100,000 and the A-body person the torture (and vice versa)—which suggests that A and B think they will be simply changing bodies: A thinks that after the process, "she" will simply be "in" the B-body person, and that's why she chooses as she does (and vice versa). However, in the second case, the person—let's say it was A—fears the proposed torture even though, if the last step is carried out, she will be exactly as the A-body person is in the first case, *for whom she chose the torture.*

So does Williams's thought experiment show that the basis of our identity is unclear? Or that our identity seems to include "both" psychological and physical elements? Or that traditional criteria such as "physical" and "psychological" aren't sufficient to account for identity?

Or does it just show that our thoughts and feelings about who and what we are are unclear and perhaps inconsistent? Or misdirected in the first case by the "neatness" or "sharpness" of the change, which was gradual in the second case? (What if, in the second case, there were a period of unconsciousness, a marked discontinuity—of ten minutes, or ten years?)

Backing up a bit, *should* the person in the second case, if she or he were thinking clearly, have feared the torture at every step proposed? Why or why not?

PERRY'S DIVIDED SELF

Brown, Jones, and Smith enter the hospital for brain rejuvenations. (In a brain rejuvenation, one's brain is removed, its circuitry is analyzed by a fabulous machine, and a new brain is put back in one's skull, just like the old one in all relevant respects, but built of healthier grey matter. After a brain rejuvenation one feels better, and may think and remember more clearly, but the memories and beliefs are not changed in content.) Their brains are removed and placed on the brain cart. The nurse accidentally overturns the cart; the brains of Brown and Smith are ruined. To conceal his tragic blunder, the nurse puts Jones's brain through the fabulous machine three times, and delivers the duplicates back to the operating room. Two of these are put in the skulls that formerly belonged to Brown and Smith. Jones's old heart has failed and, for a time, he is taken for dead.

In a few hours, however, two individuals wake up, each claiming to be Jones, each happy to be finally rid of his headaches, but somewhat upset at the drastic changes that seem to have taken place in his body. We shall call these persons "Smith-Jones" and "Brown-Jones." The question is, who are they?

Source: John Perry. "Can the Self Divide?" *Journal of Philosophy* 69.16 (1972): 463–488. 463.

Those who claim that identity is based in memory (see "Locke's Prince and Cobbler" and "Leibniz's King of China") would have to say they're both Jones. But how can they be the same person—they're doing, thinking, and feeling different things.

A further problem is that we can't say they aren't the same person (that is, that Smith-Jones is not Brown-Jones) and at the same time say that Smith-Jones is Jones and Brown-Jones is Jones. That seems to defy logic: if A is X and B is X, then A has to be B, no?

One possible solution, suggested by Perry, is to consider the *history* of a person as forming a branch; "all the person-stages thought to be of Jones plus all the post-operative stages of Smith-Jones form a branch, and all the person-stages thought to be of Jones plus all the post-operative stages of Brown-Jones form another" (471). But wouldn't this mean that before the operation, when we talked to Jones, we were not talking to a single person?

Perhaps then, we should say that all persons (even Jones before the operation) are just person-stages. So we can say that *before* the operation, Smith-Jones was Jones and Brown-Jones was Jones, and also say that *after* the operation, Smith-Jones is not Brown-Jones; that is, before the operation they were the same person, but now they're not. But then we couldn't say that future events will happen to *us*—because they'd actually happen to someone else, some other "person-stage."

So Perry suggests yet another solution: persons are lifetimes, a lifetime containing all the person-stages that are temporally related to it. Thus, each of the branches described above is a lifetime, and so too is the entire Y-shaped structure of the trunk plus its two branches. So "the pre-operative stages of Jones belong to three lifetimes: the Y-shaped structure and each of its branches" (481). Does this solution "work"?

PRICE'S *E. COLI* JOHN

Using microsurgical techniques, Smith, a Rockworth University scientist, at time t_1 dissects John, a well scrutinized *E. coli* bacterium, which, apart from being irreverently named after Rockworth's founder, is typical of its species. After isolating John's two chromosomes and its ribosomes, Smith transfers to a test tube the aqueous solution he drained from John's interior by means of a micropipette and stores the remaining cell membrane and wall in separate test tubes. Several days later, having ascertained that none of the cell parts are functioning, Smith reassembles them. An injection of substance XZ2 at time t_2 animates the reassembled cell: it thrives in a medium suitable for culturing *E. coli*'s of the same strain as John, reproduces by cell division; in brief, it exhibits all the vital properties had by living *F. coli* bacteria.

Has John continued to exist throughout?

Source: Marjorie S. Price. "Identity Through Time." *Journal of Philosophy* 74.4 (1977): 201–217. 210.

Price maintains that John *has* continued to exist and is thus challenging the view that in order to say X persists through time, there must be some description, some essential element, that applies to X throughout that time. Price claims that the only descriptions that can be applied in this way are so general (for example, "object" and "entity") that the view is rather useless. For example, perhaps the most minimal description of John is "organism" but even that does not apply throughout the entire time in question (John ceases to be an organism at some point); and yet, John continues to exist throughout that time. (Price also describes "Rover" who is sent to Mars and upon his return gradually turns into an amorphous mass of cells that can perhaps appropriately be called "Clover"—Rover ceases to be a dog, but he doesn't cease to exist.)

But if not by appealing to some essential element that continues, how can we say that John (or Rover) *does* continue to exist? Certainly *something* exists, but is it John (or Rover)? Those who claim John *doesn't* continue to exist may do so because between t_1 and t_2 there wasn't anything in existence that could be said to be identical to John, the physical bits and pieces without the organization that give rise to characteristic function being insufficient. But, counters Price, then we would also have to say that "a watch or stereo in need of repair ceases to exist when a jeweler or repairman takes it apart" (211)—in which case repairing them would be logically impossible.

So must we say that all material objects continue to exist even when they're scattered objects? (What does that option imply for the physical criterion of identity? See "Hobbes's Ship of Theseus" and "Williams's Charles and Guy Fawkes—and Robert.") Or should we "construe 'spatiotemporally continuous' in a way that allows for a spatiotemporally continuous object's occupying a discontinuous place" (211)? Or should we instead "drop spatiotemporal continuity as a necessary condition of a material object's retaining its identity over a stretch of time" (211)?

PARFIT'S FISSION

My body is fatally injured, as are the brains of my two brothers. My brain is divided, and each half is successfully transplanted into the body of one of my brothers. Each of the resulting people believes that he is me, seems to remember living my life, has my character, and is in every other way psychologically continuous with me. And he has a body that is very like mine. . . .

. . .

. . . What happens to me?

Source: Derek Parfit. *Reasons and Persons.* Oxford, UK: Oxford University Press, 1984. 254–255.

Describing first a case like Shoemaker's Brownson (see "Shoemaker's Brownson"), Parfit suggests that "you go where your brain goes"—the resulting person is Brown. Then, since it is actually possible to survive with only one functioning hemisphere (consider stroke victims), Parfit reasons also that "you go where only half your brain goes"—so if half of your brain is destroyed and the other half transplanted into another body, the resulting person is indeed you. But what if the other half is not destroyed? This is the case Parfit considers here (attributing it to David Wiggins, who modifies, in *Identity and Spatio-Temporal Continuity* (1967), Shoemaker's Brownson, postulating that Brown's brain is split and the two halves housed in two different bodies).

Parfit considers four possibilities. The first is that he does not survive. But, he reasons, since he would survive if his whole brain had been successfully transplanted and since people do survive with half their brain injured, this can't be the case. The second and third possibilities are that he survives as one or the other of the two resulting people. But if the halves are identical, why would he survive as only one—and which one? The fourth possibility is that he survives as both of the two resulting people. But one person can't be two people. (Why not? See "Parfit's Teletransporter"—what if the original you isn't lost in the replication process?)

Or, Parfit suggests, perhaps he does survive the operation and "its effect is to give me two bodies, and a divided mind" (256). In fact, people with the connection between the two hemispheres of their brains severed *do* have a divided mind, two *separate* spheres of consciousness. But, Parfit says, this "solution" involves "a great distortion in our concept of a person" (256).

Parfit then suggests that the question "Shall I be one of these two people, or the other, or neither?" is an empty question, and he argues for giving up altogether the language of identity. Identity is an all-or-nothing thing, but the things that are really important to us (like psychological connectedness) are matters of degree.

The more important, and perhaps more appropriate, question, he says, is one of survival—and he can say he survives without having to say he is one of those people. But who is it who wants to survive? (And if "who" is not important, *why* do "you" want to survive?)

Parfit's Teletransporter

Suppose that you enter a cubicle in which, when you press a button, a scanner records the states of all the cells in your brain and body, destroying both while doing so. This information is then transmitted at the speed of light to some other planet, where a replicator produces a perfect organic copy of you. Since the brain of your Replica is exactly like yours, it will seem to remember living your life up to the moment when you pressed the button, its character will be just like yours, and it will be in every other way psychologically continuous with you.

Is it you?

Source: Derek Parfit. "Divided Minds and the Nature of Persons." In *Mindwaves.* C. Blakemore and S. Greenfield, eds. London: Basil Blackwell, 1987. 19–25. 21.

Parfit uses his teletransporter to explore notions about personal identity—about what it is to be a person. One might use a physical criterion: as long as you maintain physical continuity (your body and/or brain continue to exist in space and time), you are the same person. According to this view, when you enter the teletransporter, you die, and the Replica is not you.

Or one might use a psychological criterion: as long as you maintain psychological continuity, either by maintaining memories of your past experiences (see "Leibniz's King of China") or by maintaining beliefs and desires, you are the same person. If such a continuity depends on (is caused by) continuity of the body—in particular, the brain—then again, when you enter the teletransporter, you die, and the Replica is not you. But if psychological continuity can depend on something else, such as the replication of cellular information, then you still exist—you are the Replica (or the Replica is you).

Both the physical and psychological approach (by the way, are skills such as playing a musical instrument physical or psychological?) will have to determine how much—how much of your body continues, how much you remember, how much you still believe or desire—is enough for you to still be you. But it's implausible, says Parfit, that, for example, with 51 percent you're still you, but with 49 percent you're not. Perhaps, then, instead of a certain continuing chunk of body or memory, a chain or an overlap of body parts or memories would be sufficient.

Or, as Parfit suggests, perhaps there is no you: perhaps instead of a single unified self (what we call a "person"), presumed by both approaches, "there are long series of different mental states and events—thoughts, sensations, and the like—each series being what we call one life" (20). Parfit offers the analogy of a club: "Suppose that a certain club exists for some time, holding regular meetings. The meetings then cease. Some years later, several people form a club with the same name, and the same rules" (23). To ask whether it's the same club or another but identical club is, he says, to misunderstand the nature of clubs. So is to ask "How do we decide which states and events belong to a certain series, to a certain life?" to misunderstand the nature of life?

(Given that cloning involves replication, will that technology require us to revise our concept of personal identity?)

JAMES'S SQUIRREL

[A] live squirrel [is] supposed to be clinging to one side of a tree-trunk; while over against the tree's opposite side a human being [is] imagined to stand. This human witness tries to get sight of the squirrel by moving rapidly round the tree, but no matter how fast he goes, the squirrel moves as fast in the opposite direction, and always keeps the tree between himself and the man, so that never a glimpse of him is caught. The resultant metaphysical problem now is this: *Does the man go round the squirrel or not?* He goes round the tree, sure enough, and the squirrel is on the tree; but does he go round the squirrel?

Source: William James. "What Pragmatism Means." 1907. As reprinted in *Philosophy: History and Problems.* Samuel Enoch Stumpf, ed. New York: McGraw-Hill, 1971. Book 2: 297–303. 297.

J ames uses this thought experiment to show the value of the pragmatic method (297):

> Which party is right . . . depends on what you *practically mean* by "going round" the squirrel. If you mean passing from the north of him to the east, then to the south, then to the west, and then to the north of him again, obviously the man does go round him, for he occupies these successive positions. But if on the contrary you mean being first in front of him, then on the right of him, then behind him, then on his left, and finally in front again, it is quite as obvious that the man fails to go round him, for by the compensating movements the squirrel makes, he keeps his belly turned towards the man all the time, and his back turned away.

The pragmatic method simply traces the practical consequences of a line of reasoning: "What difference would it practically make to anyone if this notion rather than that notion were true? If no practical difference whatever can be traced, then the alternatives mean practically the same thing, and all dispute is idle" (298). Such a method would, James claims, settle long-standing metaphysical disputes about whether the world is one or many, whether we have free will or not, whether things are material or not, and so on.

But do practical effects exhaust the value of a dispute? Yes, James says, referring to Charles Pierce's claim that beliefs are really just rules for action (298). But is that really all there is to belief? Can all abstract differences (in principles, definitions, and so on) be expressed by concrete differences (in facts, actions, and so on)?

James goes on to develop not only a pragmatic theory of meaning but also a pragmatic theory of truth: we have come to realize, he points out, that the natural laws theorized by science on the basis of experiment (experience) are only approximations—"no theory is absolutely a transcript of reality" (302); it follows, he says, that "ideas (which themselves are but parts of our experience) become true just in so far as they help us to get into satisfactory relation with other parts of our experience" (302, emphasis omitted). (This is in opposition to the correspondence theory of truth which claims that statements are true in so far as they correspond with reality, with the facts of our experience.) For example, James continues, "if theological ideas prove to have a value for concrete life, they will be true, for pragmatism, in the sense of being good for so much" (303, emphasis omitted). However, he adds, "for how much *more* they are true, will depend entirely on their relations to the other truths that also have to be acknowledged" (303, emphasis added). Even so, doesn't James's approach endorse delusion?

WITTGENSTEIN'S GAMES

Consider for example the proceedings that we call "games." I mean board-games, card-games, ball-games, Olympic games, and so on. What is common to them all?—Don't say: "There *must* be something common, or they would not be called 'games'"—but *look and see* whether there is anything common to all.—For if you look at them you will not see something that is common to *all*, but similarities, relationships, and a whole series of them at that. To repeat: don't think, but look!—Look for example at board games, with their multifarious relationships. Now pass to card-games; here you find many correspondences with the first group, but many common features drop out, and others appear. When we pass next to ball-games, much that is common is retained, but much is lost.—Are they all "amusing"? Compare chess with noughts and crosses. Or is there always winning and losing, or competition between players? Think of patience. In ball-games there is winning and losing; but when a child throws his ball at the wall and catches it again, this feature has disappeared. Look at the parts played by skill and luck; and at the difference between skill in chess and skill in tennis. Think now of games like ring-a-ring-a-roses; here is the element of amusement, but how many other characteristic features have disappeared! And we can go through the many, many other groups of games in the same way; can see how similarities crop up and disappear.

Source: Ludwig Wittgenstein. *Philosophical Investigations.* 1953. New York: Macmillan, 1958. Section 66.

Wittgenstein is examining here our language—specifically what our words mean. His thought experiment leads him to conclude that the standard view—that individual words name objects, that every word has a meaning—is mistaken. Instead, he says, what we find when we examine games, for example, is "a complicated network of similarities overlapping and criss-crossing" (section 66) that he calls "family resemblances" (section 67). Are the results of his experiment correct—is there no one thing all games have in common? Is his conclusion that words lack exact denotation true not just for "games" but for all our words?

One might think the lack of exact denotation makes our words meaningless, our language useless. Wittgenstein would disagree, however, claiming that a word's meaning is its use (our ways of using it), which develops over time as we live together and speak with one another (see "Wittgenstein's 'S' "). But doesn't the lack of specificity have serious implications—especially when we use words intended to denote abstractions (words like "justice," "beauty," and "truth")?

WITTGENSTEIN'S "S"

Let us imagine the following case. I want to keep a diary about the recurrence of a certain sensation. To this end I associate it with the sign "S" and write this sign in a calendar for every day on which I have the sensation.—I will remark first of all that a definition of the sign cannot be formulated.—But still I can give myself a kind of ostensive definition.—How? Can I point to the sensation? Not in the ordinary sense. But I speak, or write the sign down, and at the same time I concentrate my attention on the sensation—and so, as it were, point to it inwardly.—But what is this ceremony for? For that is all it seems to be! A definition surely serves to establish the meaning of a sign.—Well, that is done precisely by the concentrating of my attention; for in this way I impress on myself the connexion between the sign and the sensation.—But "I impress it on myself" can only mean: this process brings it about that I remember the connexion *right* in the future. But in the present case I have no criterion of correctness.

Source: Ludwig Wittgenstein. *Philosophical Investigations.* 1953. New York: Macmillan, 1958. Section 258.

Wittgenstein's thought experiment is generally understood to show that one cannot have a private language, because there would not be any previously established or objective standard against which to evaluate its correct use; such standards require a social context, a community of language users. But, one might object, why can't a solitary person *establish* a standard for determining correct use? (See "Ayer's Robinson Crusoe.")

Even so, does this inability to determine whether words are being used correctly mean, as Wittgenstein suggests (section 293), that they will have no meaning at all, that words for our private experience can't possibly be taken to *mean* anything?

> Suppose everyone had a box with something in it: we call it a "beetle." No one can look into anyone else's box, and everyone says he knows what a beetle is only by looking at *his* beetle.—Here it would be quite possible for everyone to have something different in his box. One might even imagine such a thing constantly changing. But suppose the word "beetle" had a use in these people's language?—If so it would not be used as the name of a thing. The thing in the box has no place in the language-game at all; not even as a *something:* for the box might even be empty.

So not only can we not *know* what *other people* experience (see "Locke's Inverted Spectrum"), but we can't even *talk about* what *we ourselves* experience? (Or we can, but it would be meaningless gibberish. . . .)

AYER'S ROBINSON CRUSOE

Imagine a Robinson Crusoe left alone on his island while still an infant, having not yet learned to speak. Let him, like Romulus and Remus, be nurtured by a wolf, or some other animal, until he can fend for himself; and so let him grow to manhood. He will certainly be able to recognize many things upon the island, in the sense that he adapts his behaviour to them. Is it inconceivable that he should also name them?

Source: A. J. Ayer. "Can There Be a Private Language?" *Proceedings of the Aristotelian Society* supplementary vol. 28 (1954): 63–76. 70.

Ayer believes it is *not* inconceivable that his Robinson Crusoe would name things, and he offers this thought experiment as evidence against Wittgenstein that one *can* have a private language (see "Wittgenstein's 'S' "). Wittgenstein might reply that, given our faulty memories, Ayer's Crusoe could never be sure he was following his own rules. But isn't there a difference between using a language incorrectly or inconsistently and not being able to use it at all?

Furthermore, Ayer concedes that there is a problem with endowing signs with meaning, but "it is no less of a problem in the case where the object for which the sign is supposed to stand is public than in the case where it is private" (68–69). So a private language is neither more nor less impossible than a public language.

Indeed, especially given the lack of objective standards, one could insist there *must* be a private language—if only because the subjective experience described by words can't possibly be publicly understood. That is, insofar as we use words to describe our subjective experience, which is known only to ourselves, we *necessarily* use a private language. But can that be called a language? How exactly should we define "language"?

QUINE'S GAVAGAI

[Consider] the linguist who, unaided by an interpreter, is out to penetrate and translate a language hitherto unknown. All the objective data he has to go on are the forces that he sees impinging on the native's surfaces and the observable behavior, vocal and otherwise, of the native. . . .

. . . A rabbit scurries by, the native says "Gavagai," and the linguist notes down the sentence "Rabbit" (or "Lo, a rabbit") as tentative translation, subject to testing in further cases. . . . For, suppose the native language includes . . . "Animal," "White," and "Rabbit". . . . How then is the linguist to perceive that the native would have been willing to assent to ["Animal"] in all the situations where he happened to volunteer ["Rabbit"], and in some but perhaps not all of the situations where he happened to volunteer ["White"]? Only by taking the initiative and querying combinations of native sentences and stimulus situations so as to narrow down his guesses to his eventual satisfaction.

So we have the linguist asking "Gavagai?" in each of various stimulatory situations, and noting each time whether the native assents, dissents, or neither. But how is he to recognize native assent and dissent when he sees or hears them? . . . [S]uppose that in asking "Gavagai?" and the like, in the conspicuous presence of rabbits and the like, he has elicited the responses "Evet" and "Yok" often enough to surmise that they may correspond to "Yes" and "No," but has no notion which is which.

Can the linguist ever come to know what "Gavagai" *means?*

Source: Willard Van Orman Quine. *Word and Object.* Cambridge, MA: MIT Press, 1960. 28, 29.

With this thought experiment, Quine is investigating the relationship between words and the objects they represent. He suggests that, at best, we can come to know not what "gavagai" means but only what prompts or stimulates the utterance of "gavagai." And even then, the best we can do is achieve an approximation.

One difficulty, Quine points out, is the role of prior collateral information: "[The native] may assent on the occasion of nothing better than an ill-glimpsed movement in the grass, because of his earlier observation, unknown to the linguist, of rabbits near the spot. Since the linguist would not on his own information be prompted by that same poor glimpse to assent to 'Rabbit?', we have here a discrepancy between the present stimulus meaning of 'Gavagai' for the informant and that of 'Rabbit' for the linguist. . . . [Or] there may be a local rabbit-fly, unknown to the linguist, and recognizable some way off by its long wings and erratic movements; and seeing such a fly in the neighborhood of an ill-glimpsed animal could help a native to recognize the latter as a rabbit" (37). Another difficulty, Quine says, is that "the native may dissent from 'Gavagai' in plain sight of the rabbit's ears, because the rabbit is in no position for shooting; he has misjudged the linguist's motive for asking 'Gavagai?' " (39). Furthermore, suggests Quine, maybe the objects to which "gavagai" applies are not rabbits after all, but "mere stages, or brief temporal segments, of rabbits" (51), or "undetached parts of rabbits" (52), or "the fusion . . . of all rabbits, . . . that single though discontinuous portion of the spatiotemporal world that consists of rabbits" (52), or the "recurring universal [of] rabbithood" (52)—for in all cases, what would prompt "Gavagai" would also prompt "Rabbit": "Point to a rabbit and you have pointed to a stage of a rabbit, to an integral part of a rabbit, to the rabbit fusion, and to where rabbithood is manifested" (52–53).

To determine what exactly "gavagai" means, the linguist would have to ask, while pointing, questions like "Is that one gavagai or two?"—that is, would have to know other words of the native's language. "The whole apparatus is interdependent" (53), says Quine—meaning can be determined only within the context of other meanings, within the context of the whole language.

Is the situation as "hopeless" as Quine suggests? (If we can't establish meaning in such a benign case as "gavagai" and "rabbit," where one can at least point to something, what about words that refer to abstract relationships? Imagine the linguist trying to establish the meaning of something like "Neutrinos lack mass.") Isn't learning one's first language as a child a similar case of "radical translation"—and don't we achieve more than "approximation"? (Then again, is more than approximation really necessary? See "Wittgenstein's Games.")

Putnam's Twin Earth

$[S]$uppose that some-
where in the galaxy there is a planet we shall call Twin Earth . . . [that],
apart from the differences we shall specify, . . . is *exactly* like Earth. . . .

. . .

One of the peculiarities of Twin Earth is that the liquid called "water"
is not H_2O but a different liquid whose chemical formula. . . . I shall
abbreviate . . . as XYZ. I shall suppose that XYZ is indistinguishable from
water at normal temperatures and pressures. In particular, it tastes like
water and it quenches thirst like water. Also, I shall suppose that the
oceans and lakes and seas of Twin Earth contain XYZ and not water, that
it rains XYZ on Twin Earth and not water, etc.

If a spaceship from Earth ever visits Twin Earth, then the supposition
at first will be that "water" has the same meaning on Earth and on Twin
Earth. This supposition will be corrected when it is discovered that "water" on Twin Earth is XYZ, and the Earthian spaceship will report somewhat as follows: "On Twin Earth the word 'water' means *XYZ*." . . .

Symmetrically, if a spaceship from Twin Earth ever visits Earth, then
the supposition at first will be that the word "water" has the same meaning on Twin Earth and on Earth. This supposition will be corrected when
it is discovered that "water" on Earth is H_2O, and the Twin Earthian
spaceship will report: "On Earth the word 'water' means H_2O."

. . .

Now let us roll the time back to about 1750. At that time chemistry
was not developed on either Earth or Twin Earth. The typical Earthian . . .
did not know water consisted of hydrogen and oxygen, and the typical
Twin Earthian . . . did not know "water" consisted of XYZ. Let Oscar$_1$ be

Source: Hilary Putnam. "The Meaning of Meaning." In *Minnesota Studies in the Philosophy of Science.* Vol. 7: *Language, Mind, and Knowledge.* Keith Gunderson, ed. Min-
neapolis: University of Minnesota Press, 1975. 131–193. 139–141.

such a typical Earthian . . . and let Oscar$_2$ be his counterpart on Twin Earth. You may suppose that there is no belief that Oscar$_1$ had about water that Oscar$_2$ did not have about "water" [and] that Oscar$_1$ and Oscar$_2$ were exact duplicates in appearance, feelings, thoughts, interior monologue, etc. Yet the extension [the set of things the term is true of] of the term "water" was just as much H$_2$O on Earth in 1750 as in 1950; and the extension of the term "water" was just as much XYZ on Twin Earth in 1750 as in 1950.

Will Oscar$_1$ and Oscar$_2$ understand the term "water" to have the same meaning?

The broad question Putnam is trying to answer is "What is the meaning of meaning?" A standard view of "meaning" is that "knowing the meaning of a term is just a matter of being in a certain psychological state" (135), so if two people understand a word differently, they must be in different psychological states (mental states). Putnam hopes that his Twin Earth thought experiment shows otherwise: Oscar$_1$ and Oscar$_2$ are physically identical, so when they think "water," they are in the same psychological or mental state; *however,* when they think "water," they are *not* thinking the same thing—one is thinking about H$_2$O and the other is thinking about XYZ. Thus, Putnam concludes, meaning is *not* "just in the head."

Rather, Putnam argues, meaning is determined by the external environment—the truth of the matter. In this regard, his view is decidedly realist (see "Putnam's Brain in a Vat"). And yet, because we often don't really know the truth of the matter (most of us couldn't tell whether the wet stuff we're talking about is H$_2$O or XYZ), Putnam says meaning is also determined by the sociolinguistic conventions or practices of a community. In this regard, his view is relativist. Is this a problem?

Furthermore, if neither Oscar$_1$ nor Oscar$_2$ knows chemistry, *don't* they mean the same thing when they say "water" (something like "clear tasteless thirst-quenching liquid")? Is there a difference between "mean" as in "intend" and "mean" as in "refer to"?

Lastly, does Putnam's point apply only to words for natural or material objects? What about, for example, words such as "red" and "pain"?

Descartes's Evil Demon

$\left[\text{T}\right]$here has been implanted in my mind the old opinion that there is a God who can do everything, and who made me such as I am. How do I know he has not brought it about that, while in fact there is no earth, no sky, no extended objects, no shape, no size, no place, yet all these things should appear to exist as they do now? Moreover, I judge that other men sometimes go wrong over what they think they know perfectly well; may not God likewise make me go wrong, whenever I add two and three, or count the sides of a square, or do any simpler thing that might be imagined? . . .

. . .

. . .[S]uppose then not that there is a supremely good God . . . but that there is an evil spirit, who is supremely powerful and intelligent, and does his utmost to deceive me. . . .

. . .

I suppose, therefore, that whatever things I see are illusions; I believe that none of the things my lying memory represents to have happened really did so; I have no senses; body, shape, extension, motion, place are chimeras. What then is true? . . .

Source: René Descartes. *Meditations on First Philosophy,* First and Second Meditations. 1642. As rendered in Descartes. *Philosophical Writings.* Elizabeth Anscombe and Peter Thomas Geach, trans. and eds. New York: Macmillan, 1971. 63–64, 65, 66.

In his *Meditations,* Descartes sets out to establish what he can know for sure. First, he recognizes that his senses occasionally deceive him, so sensory knowledge can't be said to be certain. Then, he admits that sometimes his dreams are so vivid, he's not sure whether he's awake or asleep—how does he know for sure he's not dreaming right now? But, he reasons, surely "whether I am awake or asleep, two and three add up to five, and a square has only four sides" (63). However, since he's set out to make a clean sweep, to be rid of old opinions and habits of thought, *to begin again from the very foundations,* he then postulates an evil demon that may be deceiving him about everything. Does his thought experiment lead him to skepticism (the view that we can't know anything about anything)? No. Instead, Descartes reasons as follows: "If he deceives me, then . . . I undoubtedly exist; let him deceive me as much as he may, he will never bring it about that, at the time of thinking . . . that I am something, I am in fact nothing. . . . 'I am,' 'I exist,' whenever I utter it or conceive it in my mind, is necessarily true" (67). Hence Descartes's famous *cogito ergo sum*—I think, therefore I am.

Having established with certainty that he exists—that he is whatever it is that's thinking, doubting, imagining—he proceeds to determine what else he can know for sure. What *does* follow from "I am"?

Backing up a bit, *can* he be sure he exists? And *can* he be sure the thinking thing is an "I"? (And if so, where is it? See "Putnam's Brain in a Vat.") Could it be a "we"? Or an "it"? Or just the "thinking"?

RUSSELL'S FIVE-MINUTE HYPOTHESIS

There is no logical impossibility in the hypothesis that the world sprang into being five minutes ago, exactly as it then was, with a population that "remembered" a wholly unreal past.

Source: Bertrand Russell. *The Analysis of Mind.* 1921. London: George Allen & Unwin, 1968. 159.

Russell presented his "five-minute hypothe-sis" merely to show that memories of something are logically independent of actual occurrences of that something. And despite his comments that the hypothesis is uninteresting as support for skepticism (the view that we cannot know anything about anything), philosophers have used it for that very purpose. One might respond to such skeptics by suggesting that the hypothesis could be disproved by, for example, pointing to a newspaper dated yesterday or to one's faded and worn jeans. But, the skeptics will re-spond, the universe could've been created five minutes ago *to look as if* it had existed for any number of years. So is the five-minute hypothesis "as good as" the six-billion-year hypothesis? (If not, why not?)

PLATO'S EQUAL PORTIONS OF WOOD AND STONE

[W]hat would you say of equal portions of wood and stone, or other material equals? . . . Are they equals in the same sense in which absolute equality is equal? Or do they fall short of this perfect equality in a measure?

[Simmias replies they fall short of absolute equality.]

. . .

Then we must have known equality previously to the time when we first saw the material equals, and reflected that all these apparent equals strive to attain absolute equality, but fall short of it?

[Simmias agrees.]

. . .

Then before we began to see or hear or perceive in any way, we must have had a knowledge of absolute equality, or we could not have referred to that standard the equals which are derived from the senses?

Source: Plato. *Phaedo.* c. 380 BCE. B. Jowett, trans. Roslyn, NY: Walter J. Black, 1942. 107.

Plato shows in this thought experiment that we could not possibly have derived the idea of absolute equality from sense experience alone, since none of the "equal" portions of wood, stone, and so on that we perceive with our senses are absolutely equal. The idea of absolute equality must therefore be innate (a fundamental idea or principle built into the mind itself or, as Plato actually suggests, learned prior to birth and then later remembered in the presence of certain stimuli)—since we do, in fact, *have* the idea. (Other innate ideas are, Plato suggests, beauty, goodness, and justice.) But *is* it the case that we do not gain the idea of absolute equality from sense experience? And if so, does that prove that we have innate ideas? (See "Mill's Chaotic World.")

DESCARTES'S WAX

Consider . . . this wax. It has just been extracted from the honeycomb; it has not completely lost the taste of the honey; it retains some of the smell of the flowers from which it was gathered; its colour, shape, size are manifest; it is hard, cold, and easily handled, and gives out a sound if you rap it with your knuckle; in fact it has all the properties that seem to be needed for our knowing a body with the utmost distinctness. But while I say this, the wax is put by the fire. It loses the remains of its flavour, the fragrance evaporates, the colour changes, the shape is lost, the size increases, it becomes fluid and hot, it can hardly be handled, and it will no longer give you a sound if you rap it. Is the same wax, then, still there?

Source: René Descartes. *Meditations on First Philosophy,* Second Meditation. 1642. As rendered in Descartes. *Philosophical Writings.* Elizabeth Anscombe and Peter Thomas Geach, trans. and eds. New York: Macmillan, 1971. 72.

Descartes's answer is "Of course it is." But—and this is the interesting part—if we know it's the same wax, still there, then we can't know by perception or sensory experience, because "whatever fell under taste, smell, sight, touch, or hearing has now changed" (72). How then do we know?

And is this thought experiment applicable to all our knowing?

MOLYNEUX'S BLIND MAN

Suppose a man *born* blind, and now adult, and taught by his *touch* to distinguish between a cube and a sphere of the same metal, and nighly of the same bigness, so as to tell, when he felt one and the other, which is the cube, which the sphere. Suppose then the cube and sphere placed on a table, and the blind man be made to see: *quaere*, whether *by his sight, before he touched them,* he could now distinguish and tell which is the globe, which the cube?

Source: William Molyneux. In a letter dated 1693 to John Locke, quoted by Locke in the second edition (1694) of *An Essay Concerning Human Understanding.* Book 2, Chapter 9, Section 8. As collated and annotated by Alexander Campbell Fraser. New York: Dover, 1959. Volume 1. 186–187.

Molyneux predicts that the man could *not* distinguish between the globe and the cube by sight alone because he hasn't had the necessary experience; he hasn't learned how visual perceptions relate to physical realities. Molyneux believes his thought experiment disproves the existence of innate ideas (see "Plato's Equal Portions of Wood and Stone") that are argued to exist by rationalists (usually on the basis of universal agreement on certain principles); rationalists would say the man *would* be able to recognize and distinguish the globe and cube, by matching what he now sees with the ideas he has of them in his mind—ideas he has always had, independent of his experience through life. Empiricists such as Molyneux and Locke, however, say we are not *born* with such ideas, with such knowledge about the physical world; rather, when we are born, as Locke says, our minds are a *tabula rasa* (a blank tablet) and we *acquire* knowledge through sensory experience and the subsequent reasoning of association and abstraction. Is Molyneux correct in his prediction—and its implication?

Contemporary philosopher Janet Levin modifies Molyneux's experiment (in "Could Love Be like a Heatwave?"), postulating that if the man had learned, while blind, geometric facts about three-dimensional figures and had heard statements about such figures made by sighted people, and then, when newly sighted, had been shown other geometrical figures and told what they were, he *would* be able to distinguish between the globe and cube. If that is so, what are the implications for how we know what we know?

Hume's Missing Shade of Blue

Suppose . . . a person to have enjoyed his sight for thirty years, and to have become perfectly acquainted with colors of all kinds except one particular shade of blue, for instance, which it never has been his fortune to meet with. Let all the different shades of that color, except that single one, be placed before him, descending gradually from the deepest to the lightest; it is plain that he will perceive a blank, where that shade is wanting, and will be sensible that there is a greater distance in that place between the contiguous colors than in any other. Now I ask, whether it be possible for him, from his own imagination, to supply this deficiency, and raise up to himself the idea of that particular shade, though it had never been conveyed to him by his senses?

Source: David Hume. *An Enquiry Concerning Human Understanding.* Section 2. 1748. As reprinted in *The English Philosophers from Bacon to Mill.* Edwin A. Burtt, ed. New York: Random House, 1939. 592–596. 595.

Hume says it *is* possible, which shows that our thoughts do *not* depend on what we have experienced—which supports the rationalist view (we have ideas that are preexistent to or independent of our experience, and we can acquire knowledge by reasoning alone).

However, Hume is actually an empiricist (see "Molyneux's Blind Man"); as a general rule, he says, "[the] creative power of the mind amounts to no more than the faculty of compounding, transposing, augmenting, or diminishing the materials afforded us by the senses and experience" (594). If we analyze what we can imagine or think about, he says, we'll see that our ideas are just combinations of elements we've experienced (we can imagine a gold mountain, for example, because we have been previously acquainted with gold and mountains); furthermore, he says, people unable to experience a certain element will not be able to think of it (for example, a deaf person can't imagine the sound of a trumpet). Color, he says, is an exception that may prove that it's not "absolutely impossible" for ideas to arise independent of sense experience.

Is color an exception (see "Jackson's Mary, the Brilliant Color Scientist"), and if so, why? Or is our ability to imagine the missing shade (*are* we actually able to imagine it?) just, as in other cases, a compounding of what we've experienced—we just combine blue and white (or whatever) in the right amounts to imagine that missing shade. Perhaps a better test to settle the rationalist-empiricist debate is to ask "Can we imagine the brand new color 'prillany'?"

Hume's Constant Conjunction

Suppose a person . . . endowed with the strongest faculties of reason and reflection [were] to be brought on a sudden into this world; he would, indeed, immediately observe a continual success of objects, and one event following another; but he would not be able to discover anything farther. He would not, at first, by any reasoning, be able to reach the idea of cause and effect; since the particular powers, by which all natural operations are performed, never appear to the senses; nor is it reasonable to conclude, merely because one event, in one instance, precedes another, that therefore the one is the cause, the other the effect. Their conjunction may be arbitrary and casual. There may be no reason to infer the existence of one from the appearance of the other. And in a word, such a person, without more experience, could never employ his conjecture or reasoning concerning any matter of fact, or be assured of anything beyond what was immediately present to his memory and senses.

Suppose, again, that he has acquired more experience, and has lived so long in the world as to have observed familiar objects or events to be constantly conjoined together; what is the consequence of this experience? He immediately infers the existence of one object from the appearance of the other. Yet he has not, by all his experience, acquired any idea or knowledge of the secret power by which the one object produces the other; nor is it, by any process of reasoning [the case that] he is engaged to draw this inference. But still he finds himself determined to draw it: And though he should be convinced that his understanding has no part in the operation, he would nevertheless continue in the same course of thinking. There is some other principle which determines him to form such a conclusion.

Source: David Hume. *An Enquiry Concerning Human Understanding.* Section 5, Part 1. 1748. As reprinted in *The English Philosophers from Bacon to Mill.* Edwin A. Burtt, ed. New York: Random House, 1967. 585–689. 609.

This other principle, says Hume, is custom or habit: "After the constant conjunction of two objects—heat and flame, for instance, weight and solidity—we are determined by custom alone to expect the one from the appearance of the other" (610); after all, we can't actually *see* the causal connection. Whether we draw an inference from one instance or from a thousand instances, it is the same inference; that what we observe happens a thousand times makes it no more causally necessary than if it happens only once. So instead of knowledge and understanding, all we have is probability. "All inferences from experience," Hume says, "are effects of custom, not of reasoning" (610).

But *would* Hume's person—"with the strongest faculties of reason and reflection"—be, as he says, unable to discover or establish cause and effect from experience?

KANT'S *A PRIORI* SPACE

Take away . . . from the concept of a body, as supplied by experience, everything that is empirical, one by one; such as colour, hardness or softness, weight, and even impenetrability, and there still remains the space which the body (now entirely vanished) occupied: that you cannot take away. . . . Convinced, therefore, by the necessity with which that concept forces itself upon you, you will have to admit that it has its seat in your faculty of knowledge *a priori.*

Source: Immanuel Kant. *Critique of Pure Reason.* 1781. F. Max Müller, trans. Garden City, NY: Anchor Books, 1966. 4–5.

Investigating reason and what it can know independent of sense experience, Kant advocates both empiricism and rationalism: knowledge is not only *a posteriori* (arrived at through empirical investigation), but also *a priori* (arrived at by reason, or reasoning, independent of sense experience). "If we remove from experience everything that belongs to the senses," Kant says, "there remain nevertheless certain original concepts [such as the concept of space], and certain judgments derived from them, which must have had their origin entirely *a priori* and independent of all experience" (1). It is through these built-in concepts that we organize or process our experience.

But *does* Kant's thought experiment yield the results he expects? That is, *is* it impossible to imagine away space? (Are there any other built-in concepts, additional to or instead of space, that our mind seems to have come equipped with?) Or do we "know" space only because of our sensory experience of the world? (See "Strawson's No-Space World.")

(And would we know *anything* if we had *no senses at all?*) (If we had no reason at all?)

MILL'S CHAOTIC WORLD

Were we to suppose . . . that the present order of the universe were brought to an end, and that a chaos succeeded in which there was no fixed succession of events, and the past gave no assurance of the future; if a human being were miraculously kept alive to witness this change, he surely would soon cease to believe in any uniformity, the uniformity itself no longer existing. If this be admitted, the belief in uniformity either is not an instinct, or it is an instinct conquerable, like all other instincts, by acquired knowledge.

Source: John Stuart Mill. *A System of Logic.* Book 3, Chapter 21, Section 1. 1843. J. M. Robson, ed. Toronto: University of Toronto Press, 1973. 565–566.

And since, according to Mill, it is from the many "uniformities of sequence" in our world that we have generalized the universality of cause and effect (see "Hume's Constant Conjunction"), he is suggesting with this thought experiment not merely that a belief in uniformity is not an instinct (or an innate idea—see "Plato's Equal Portions of Wood and Stone"), but that the law of causality is not an instinct or innate idea. Rather, Mill argues, it is a habit of thought, an induction (a generalization based on particulars), formed by our experience of the world.

Can other supposed innate ideas be disproved in a similar fashion? (See "Kant's *A Priori* Space.")

Gettier's Smith and Jones (and Brown in Barcelona)

Suppose that Smith and Jones have applied for a certain job. And suppose that Smith has strong evidence for the following conjunctive proposition: (d) Jones is the man who will get the job, and Jones has ten coins in his pocket. Smith's evidence for (d) might be that the president of the company assured him that Jones would in the end be selected, and that he, Smith, had counted the coins in Jones's pocket ten minutes ago. Proposition (d) entails: (e) The man who will get the job has ten coins in his pocket. Let us suppose that Smith sees the entailment from (d) to (e), and accepts (e) on the grounds of (d), for which he has strong evidence. In this case, Smith is clearly justified in believing that (e) is true.

But imagine, further, that unknown to Smith, he himself, not Jones, will get the job. And, also, unknown to Smith, he himself has ten coins in his pocket. Proposition (e) is then true, though proposition (d), from which Smith inferred (e), is false.

Does Smith *know* that the man who will get the job has ten coins in his pocket?

Source: Edmund L. Gettier. "Is Justified True Belief Knowledge?" *Analysis* 23.6 (1963). 121–123. 122. Copyright © 1963 Blackwell Publishing. Reprinted by permission.

Gettier is challenging the standard account of knowledge, which says that one knows X if (1) one believes X to be true, (2) one is justified in believing X to be true, and (3) X is indeed true. Smith *believes* it is true that the man who will get the job has ten coins in his pocket; he is *justified* in believing it to be true (on the basis of the president's assurance and his counting Jones's coins and his then "putting two and two together"); and it is indeed *true* that the man who will get the job has ten coins in his pocket. Nevertheless, Gettier suggests, it is clear that Smith does not *know* that the man who will get the job has ten coins in his pocket (for it is Smith himself who gets the job and not, as he had thought, Jones—and he didn't know that he himself had ten coins in his pocket). So what's wrong with the standard account?

In a similar case, Gettier shows that the problem (a justified belief happening to be true even though it was derived by using what turns out to be a false premise) can arise not only with conjunctive propositions (those involving "and") but also with disjunctive propositions (those involving "or"). Let us suppose, says Gettier, that Smith has strong evidence for the proposition "Jones owns a Ford"; Smith may then correctly infer "Either Jones owns a Ford, or Brown is in Barcelona" on the basis of that preceding proposition (for which he has strong evidence), so he would be completely justified in believing the Barcelona proposition—even though he has no idea where Brown is. Imagine, however, continues Gettier, that Jones does *not* own a Ford (he sold it just yesterday on the spur of the moment) and that, by sheer coincidence, Brown *is* in Barcelona. Surely, says Gettier, contrary to the standard account, Smith cannot have claimed to know that "Either Jones owns a Ford, or Brown is in Barcelona." (But why not, exactly?)

Skyrms's Pyromaniac

A pyromaniac has just purchased a box of Sure-Fire Matches. He has done so many times before, and has noted that they have always lit when struck unless they were wet. Furthermore, he has a certain rudimentary knowledge of chemistry—enough for him to know that oxygen must be present for things to burn and enough to assure him that the observed regularity between matches' being struck and their lighting is not merely a spurious correlation. He ascertains that the matches are dry and that there is plenty of oxygen present. He now proceeds to strike the match, confident in the belief that it will light. It does. . . . But let us assume that unbeknownst to our friend, certain impurities got into this match at the factory which raised its combustion temperature above the temperature that could be attained by friction when it is struck. Assume further than an extremely rare burst of Q-radiation happened to arrive at the very time and place the match was being struck, igniting it, and enabling our friend to accomplish his purpose.

Did the pyromaniac *know* the match would light?

Source: Brian Skyrms. "The Explication of 'X Knows That *p.*'" *Journal of Philosophy* 64.12 (1966): 373–389. 383.

Skyrms is investigating the role of cause in the relation between belief, justification, and truth with regard to claims of knowledge. The pyromaniac *believes* the matches will light. His belief is *justified* by his knowledge and his past experience with Sure-Fire Matches. And, it turns out, his justified belief is *true,* because the match does indeed light. But, says Skyrms, we wouldn't say the pyromaniac *knew* the match would light. Why not? Like the Gettier cases (see "Gettier's Smith and Jones (and Brown in Barcelona)"), the pyromaniac's claim to know *X* involves an inference, but unlike the Gettier cases, in this case the beliefs upon which the pyromaniac bases his knowledge are true (in the Gettier cases, the company president's statement to Smith was false and Jones did not own a Ford). Even so, we still don't want to say the pryromaniac *knew,* do we?

Skyrms suggests that in this case, the basis for justification isn't what *made* the belief true: it wasn't the pyromaniac's knowledge of chemistry and past experience but the timely presence of Q-radiation that resulted in his belief being true; his knowledge and past experience turned out to be insufficient because of the impurities in the match (that is, insufficient to "cause" truth, not insufficient to warrant justification). So it seems a causal connection between truth and justification is required (the justification must "make" the belief true) before one can make a claim to knowledge. Is that so for all cases in which we want to say we *know* something? And what sort of causal connection? How strong a causal connection?

Harman's False Report

A political leader is assassinated. His associates, fearing a coup, decide to pretend that the bullet hit someone else. On nationwide television they announce that an assassination attempt has failed to kill the leader but has killed a secret service man by mistake. However, before the announcement is made, an enterprising reporter on the scene telephones the real story to his newspaper, which has included the story in its final edition. Jill buys a copy of that paper and reads the story of the assassination. What she reads is true and so are her assumptions about how the story came to be in the paper. The reporter, whose by-line appears, saw the assassination and dictated his report, which is now printed just as he dictated it.

Does Jill *know* that the political leader has been assassinated?

Source: Gilbert Harman. *Thought.* Princeton, NJ: Princeton University Press, 1973. 143.

On the one hand, Jill's belief is true (the political leader has been assassinated) and justified (the newspaper report can be trusted), and so it would seem she does know. On the other hand, as Harman points out, everyone else has heard the televised announcement that claimed the assassination attempt failed, and if they also read the newspaper story, they may well not know what to believe; "it is highly implausible," Harman says, "that Jill should know simply because she lacks evidence everyone else has" (144). So, Harman concludes, "her knowledge is undermined by evidence she does not possess" (144)—for if Jill had known about the televised announcement, her belief that the political leader had been assassinated would've been unjustified, or at least less justified than it otherwise was. But how can what you *don't* know (especially if what you don't know is false) "weaken" your claim to know what you *do* know?

Harman's thought experiment leads him to consider qualifying the justification requirement of knowledge: "One knows only if there is no evidence such that if one knew about the evidence one would not be justified in believing one's conclusion" (146). Is this condition sufficient qualification? (See "Goldman's Fake Barns.") What would count as such undermining evidence?

GOLDMAN'S FAKE BARNS

Henry is driving in the countryside with his son. For the boy's edification, Henry identifies various objects on the landscape as they come into view. "That's a cow," says Henry. "That's a tractor," "That's a silo," "That's a barn," etc. Henry has no doubt about the identity of these objects; in particular, he has no doubt that the last-mentioned object is a barn, which indeed it is. Each of the identified objects has features characteristic of its type. Moreover, each object is fully in view, Henry has excellent eyesight, and he has enough time to look at them reasonably carefully, since there is little traffic to distract him.

Given this information, would we say that Henry *knows* that the object is a barn? Most of us would have little hesitation in saying this, so long as we were not in a certain philosophical frame of mind. Contrast our inclination here with the inclination we would have if we were given some additional information. Suppose we are told that, unknown to Henry, the district he has just entered is full of papier-mâché facsimiles of barns. These facsimiles look from the road exactly like barns, but are really just façades, without back walls or interiors, quite incapable of being used as barns. They are so cleverly constructed that travelers invariably mistake them for barns. Having just entered the district, Henry has not encountered any facsimiles; the object he sees is a genuine barn. But if the object on that site were a facsimile, Henry would mistake it for a barn. Given this new information, we would be strongly inclined to withdraw the claim that Henry *knows* the object is a barn. How is this change in our assessment to be explained?

Source: Alvin I. Goldman. "Discrimination and Perceptual Knowledge." *Journal of Philosophy* 73.20 (1976): 771–791. 772–773.

Goldman is exploring with this thought experiment the traditional account of knowledge as justified true belief. In both cases, Henry's belief is justified and true, so there must be some other element that distinguishes knowing (the first case) from not knowing (the second case). That element can't be cause since in both cases, Henry's belief was "caused" by the same thing, the presence of the barn (see "Skyrms's Pyromaniac"). We could, of course, back up and say that in both cases, Henry *does* know (why?) or in both cases, he doesn't (why?). But Goldman persists in his analysis that in the first, he does, and in the second, he doesn't.

Goldman initially considers that, unlike in the first case, in the second case, Henry was *accidentally* right—but Goldman isn't convinced that being accidentally right is a sufficient criterion for evaluating claims of knowledge in all cases.

He next considers that, again unlike in the first case, in the second case, there is some condition (the presence of papier-mâché barns) that would defeat his justification (see "Harman's False Report"). However, Goldman reasons, this approach seems to rule out too much, for wouldn't it be possible in almost every case to imagine some condition that, if true, would defeat one's justification for claiming *X*? Is there some way to limit the definition of "defeat" to make it usable?

Goldman moves on, suggesting that one knows *X* when one can distinguish true *X* from false *X*. In the first case, there are no fake barns (false *X*s), so, rather by default, we say Henry knows it's a barn. However, in the second case, Henry would not be able to tell the real barn from a fake one, so he doesn't really know when he says it's a barn. Is Goldman's analysis adequate? Can it be applied to all claims of knowledge? For example, if Henry can tell a dog from a cat, is that sufficient? Or must he be able to tell a dog from a wolf? (And must the dog be a wolfish-looking Malamute or can it be a decidedly un-wolfish-looking Dachshund?) And does it matter *how* he tells the difference (for example, whether by logical reasoning, or irrational induction, or a lucky guess)? (And, since a motion sensor light can discriminate between moving objects and stationary objects and, as a result, turns on when you approach, does it *know* you're approaching?)

Bonjour's Clairvoyants

Samantha believes herself to have the power of clairvoyance, though she has no reasons for or against this belief. One day she comes to believe, for no apparent reason, that the President is in New York City. She maintains this belief, appealing to her alleged clairvoyant power, even though she is at the same time aware of a massive amount of apparently cogent evidence, consisting of news reports, press releases, allegedly live television pictures, etc., indicating that the President is at that time in Washington, D.C. Now the President is in fact in New York City, the evidence to the contrary being part of a massive official hoax mounted in the face of an assassination threat. Moreover, Samantha does in fact have completely reliable clairvoyant power, under the conditions that were then satisfied, and her belief about the President did result from the operation of that power.

Does Samantha *know* the President is in New York City?

Source: Laurence Bonjour. "Externalist Theories of Empirical Knowledge." *Midwest Studies in Philosophy* 5 (1980): 53–75. 59–60.

The standard account is that in order to qualify as knowledge, one's beliefs must be justified and true. But does "justified" mean that *the person* has good reason for believing X or just that there *is* good reason for believing X? Bonjour's thought experiment challenges those who hold the latter view, a view that implies that one can be said to know X even though one has no good reason for believing X and/or even though one has good reason for *not* believing X. Samantha has no good reason for believing she is clairvoyant and thus no good reason for believing the president is in New York City; further, she has good reason for *not* believing the president is in New York City (news reports claiming he is in Washington). Bonjour says she is, therefore, "thoroughly irrational and irresponsible in disregarding cogent evidence that the President is not in New York City on the basis of a clairvoyant power which she has no reason at all to think that she possesses" (60). Her irrationality is not canceled by the fact that she's right, says Bonjour, and it is her irrationality that prevents her claim from being justified—Samantha cannot be said to know that the president is in New York City.

Bonjour postulates another clairvoyant, Norman, who, like Samantha, has no good reason for believing he is clairvoyant; unlike Samantha, however, he does *not* have good reason for not believing the president is in New York City (there is no evidence indicating, for example, that he is in Washington)—so when *he* says the president is in New York, he's not ignoring evidence to the contrary. Is he nevertheless being irrational (and therefore unjustified in his belief)? Is it irrational to believe X for no reason? If so, how good a reason is good enough? Does it depend on the person? On the X?

PLANTINGA'S EPISTEMICALLY INFLEXIBLE CLIMBER

[C]onsider the Case of the Epistemically Inflexible Climber. Ric is climbing Guide's Wall, on Storm Point in the Grand Tetons; having just led the difficult next to last pitch, he is seated on a comfortable ledge, bringing his partner up. He believes that Cascade Canyon is down to his left, that the cliffs of Mount Owen are directly in front of him, that there is a hawk gliding in lazy circles 200 feet below him, that he is wearing his new *Fire* rock shoes, and so on. His beliefs, we may stipulate, are coherent. Now add that Ric is struck by a wayward burst of high-energy cosmic radiation. This induces a cognitive malfunction; his beliefs become fixed, no longer responsive to changes in experience. No matter what his experience, his beliefs remain the same. At the cost of considerable effort his partner gets him down and, in a desperate last-ditch attempt at therapy, takes him to the opera in nearby Jackson, where the New York Metropolitan Opera on tour is performing *La Traviata*. Ric is appeared to in the same way as everyone else there; he is inundated by wave after wave of golden sound. Sadly enough, the effort at therapy fails; Ric's beliefs remain fixed and wholly unresponsive to his experience; he still believes that he is on the belay ledge at the top of the next to last pitch of Guide's Wall, that Cascade Canyon is down to his left, that there is a hawk sailing in lazy circles 200 feet below him, that he is wearing his new *Fire* rock shoes, and so on. Furthermore, since he believes the very same things he believed when seated on the ledge, his beliefs are coherent.

Are Ric's postradiation beliefs justified?

Source: Alvin Plantinga. *Warrant: The Current Debate.* New York: Oxford University Press, 1993. 82.

Plantinga uses this thought experiment to challenge the coherence theory of knowledge, which says that a belief is justified as long as it is coherent (consistent) with other beliefs (in the relevant system or structure of belief). According to the coherence theory, Ric's beliefs *are* justified. But, Plantinga claims, because his beliefs are "not appropriately responsive to his experience" (82), they are *not* justified; "coherence," Plantinga concludes, "is not sufficient for positive epistemic status" (82). Nor is it necessary, Plantinga goes on to say: we are often justified in believing something that "doesn't fit" with the rest of our beliefs. Nevertheless, Plantinga does not reject coherence altogether: it may simply be one source among many (others being experience and reason) providing epistemic justification for belief.

An interesting question might be "Which source 'trumps' the others when conflicts arise?" For example, what if your reason tells you to believe one thing but your experience tells you to believe another? (And one of those beliefs is coherent with the rest of your beliefs.)

LEHRER'S MR. TRUETEMP

Suppose a person, Mr. Truetemp, undergoes brain surgery by an experimental surgeon who invents a small device that is both a very accurate thermometer and a computational device capable of generating thoughts. The device, call it a tempucomp, is implanted in Truetemp's head so that the very tip of the device, no larger than the head of a pin, sits unnoticed on his scalp and acts as a sensor to transmit information about the temperature to the computational system in his brain. This device, in turn, sends a message to his brain causing him to think of the temperature recorded by the external sensor. Assume that the tempucomp is very reliable, and so his thoughts are correct temperature thoughts. All told, this is a reliable belief-forming process and a properly functioning cognitive faculty.

Now imagine, finally, that Mr. Truetemp has no idea that the tempucomp has been inserted in his brain and is only slightly puzzled about why he thinks so obsessively about the temperature; but he never checks a thermometer to determine whether these thoughts about the temperature are correct. He accepts them unreflectively, another effect of the tempucomp. Thus, he thinks and accepts that the temperature is 104 degrees. It is. Does he know that it is?

Source: Keith Lehrer. *Theory of Knowledge.* 1990. Boulder, CO: Westview Press, 2000. 163–164.

Lehrer is examining an epistemological position known as externalism, which says that in order for true belief to count as knowledge, there must an appropriate connection between belief and truth. What counts as "an appropriate connection"? One possibility is that the belief be formed according to a reliable cognitive process or properly functioning cognitive faculty. (What counts as "a reliable cognitive process" or "properly functioning cognitive faculty"?) But, Lehrer asks with this thought experiment, what if the person has no idea how his or her beliefs are formed? Then, suggests Lehrer, the person can't be said to *know:* "Does [Mr. Truetemp] know that the temperature is 104 degrees when the thought occurs to him while strolling in Pima Canyon? He has no idea why the thought occurred to him or that such thoughts are almost always correct. He does not, consequently, know that the temperature is 104 degrees when that thought occurs to him" (187). How knowledgeable must we be about our cognitive processes? And if knowledge about our cognitive processes is obtained *through* those cognitive processes, how can it be knowledge?

Another possibility is that the belief is formed on the basis of a reliable third-person source (see "Gettier's Smith and Jones (and Brown in Barcelona)"). How do we determine its reliability? (Especially if our own cognitive processes or faculties are unreliable?) And how reliable must the source be?

THE LIAR PARADOX

Suppose Epimenides of Crete says to you "Cretans are always liars." Is that true or false?

Source: Attributed to Epimenides by Plato, c. 500 BCE.

If what Epimenides (a Cretan) says is false (and so Cretans are not always liars), then what he says could well be true, but if what he says is true (that all Cretans are liars), then what he says is false (it's a lie). But doesn't logic tell us that a statement can't be both true and false? So do we reject logic?

Whether or not Cretans always lie can be determined empirically. And whether or not Epimenides said "Cretans are always liars" can be determined empirically. And the truth or falseness of the first is not dependent on the truth or falseness of the second. So, if it turns out, based on empirical investigation (and not on Epimenides' say-so), that Cretans do *not* always lie, then Epimenides lied when he said they do. No problem. But what if it turns out that they *do* always lie? Then Epimenides lied. But then that would mean Cretans do *not* always lie. . . .

Perhaps there is something about being "true" and "false" that we need to reject or revise? (See "The Barber Paradox.")

THE BARBER PARADOX

Imagine a village in which a barber (a man) is to shave all and only those men in the village who don't shave themselves. Does the barber shave himself?

Source: Of unknown and ancient origin, but popularized by Bertrand Russell (in *Principia Mathematica*).

If the barber doesn't shave himself, then he falls into the category of men he is to shave—so he does shave himself. But if he does shave himself, then he's *not* in the category of men he is to shave—so he doesn't shave himself. Again, is there something wrong with logic? Is there something wrong with the scenario as described?

Both the Barber and the Liar (see "The Liar Paradox") are examples of what's called "the paradox of self-reference." The logical impossibility arises in both cases because the description, the statement, refers to itself. But why should that be a problem? (Perhaps the problem is one of perspective—perhaps there's something "illegitimate" about self-reference, like looking at yourself *from* the mirror.) And, what's the solution?

FREGE'S OTHER-THINKING BEINGS

[W]hat if beings were . . . found whose laws of thought flatly contradicted ours and therefore frequently led to contrary results even in practice? . . . [W]ho is right? Whose laws of taking-to-be-true are in accord with the laws of truth?

Source: Gottlob Frege. *The Basic Laws of Arithmetic: Exposition of the System.* 1893. Montgomery Furth, trans. Berkeley: University of California Press, 1964. 14.

The laws of logic, says Frege, lead one to truth, and the truth of the matter—whether it's "2 + 2 = 4" or "X is hungry"—is not relative to where, or when, or by whom it is claimed. So, Frege would say, if such beings were to claim that 2 + 2 = 5, they'd simply be wrong; and if their claim had been "correctly" derived from their laws of thought, then those laws of thought would be wrong.

But couldn't we say instead that there are different systems of thought—different logics? How could that be? What laws of thought would a different logic have? (For example, what laws of thought would result in "2 + 2 = 5"?) Would such laws still be logical?

And would they still be related to truth? (What is truth? Are there different truths?)

THE SURPRISE QUIZ

Suppose a professor announces "Some day this term, there will be a surprise quiz." And suppose a few students reason as follows. The quiz can't be given on the last day of the term because if it hadn't been given before then, it would have to be given on that last day—in which case they'd expect it and it wouldn't be a surprise. Nor can it be given on the second last day because, again, if it hadn't been given before then, it would have to be given on that second last day (since the last day is out of the question, as they just reasoned)—in which case, again, they'd expect it and it wouldn't be a surprise. And so on for the third last day, and the fourth last day. . . . They conclude that a surprise quiz can't be given. Are they right? Is it impossible for the professor to give a surprise quiz?

Source: The original version of this paradox involved an unexpected civic defense drill (rather than an unexpected examination) and is attributed to Lennart Ekbom, who developed it sometime between 1939 and 1945; another popular version involves the day a condemned person is to be hung.

The surprise quiz paradox has puzzled philosophers for some time and many "solutions" have been offered. One suggestion is that if the quiz is given on the last day, would it not have been unexpected (that is, a surprise) *up to* the day before? And indeed, if it is given on any day other than the last day, would it not be unexpected on *that* particular day? Does this solve the paradox or just avoid it?

Another solution draws attention to circularity: concluding that the quiz could not be given on the last day requires as a premise that it not be given on the second last day, but then concluding that it could not be given on the second last day requires as a premise that it not be given on the last day—so at that point, one presumes exactly what one is trying to prove (that it not be given on the last day). Is that a correct assessment, and hence solution, of the problem?

Other solutions may be suggested by considering that if the professor says "Some day this term, there will be a surprise quiz—and today's the day!" (and she proceeds to give the quiz), then it is indeed a surprise. So it appears that there is a problem only if the announcement is made on a day prior to the day of the quiz—why is that?

BLACK'S TWO SPHERES

Isn't it logically possible that the universe [could have] contained nothing but two exactly similar spheres? We might suppose that each was made of chemically pure iron and had a diameter of one mile, that they had the same temperature, color, and so on, and that nothing else existed. Then every quality and relational characteristic of the one would also be a property of the other. Now if what I am describing is logically possible, it is not impossible for two things to have all their properties in common.

Source: Max Black. "Identity of Indiscernibles." *Mind* 61 (1952): 153–164. 156.

This thought experiment is designed by Black as an attempt to refute the principle of identity of indiscernibles, which basically says that if two things are indiscernible (they have all the same properties and no different properties), then they are actually the same one thing; that is, there can't *be* two things with *exactly all* the same properties.

One might suggest that the two spheres *are* discernible, if only because they occupy different places in space—hence, the thought experiment fails. However, such a response presumes the presence of a third object, a reference point against which to establish the "objective" location of each sphere. If there is nothing in the universe except the two spheres, as the experiment stipulates, then their locations can be established only in relation to each other, and such locations would be identical (for example, each sphere is two miles from the center of another sphere). So does the thought experiment succeed?

GOODMAN'S GRUE

Suppose that all emeralds examined before a certain time t are green. At time t, then, our observations support the hypothesis that all emeralds are green; and this is in accord with our definition of confirmation. Our evidence statements assert that emerald a is green, that emerald b is green, and so on; and each confirms the general hypothesis that all emeralds are green. So far, so good.

Now let me introduce another predicate less familiar than "green." It is the predicate "grue" and it applies to all things examined before t [that] are green [and all things examined after t that] are blue. Then at time t we have, for each evidence statement asserting that a given emerald is green, a parallel evidence statement asserting that that emerald is grue. And the statements that emerald a is grue, that emerald b is grue, and so on, will each confirm the general hypothesis that all emeralds are grue. Thus according to our definition, the prediction that all emeralds subsequently examined will be green and the prediction that all will be grue are alike confirmed by evidence statements describing the same observations. But if an emerald subsequently examined is grue, it is blue and hence not green. Thus although we are well aware which of the two incompatible predictions is genuinely confirmed, they are equally well confirmed according to our present definition.

Source: Nelson Goodman. *Fact, Fiction, and Forecast.* 4th ed. Cambridge, MA: Harvard University Press, 1983. 73.

Philosophers have traditionally distinguished between deduction (reasoning from generals to particulars) and induction (reasoning from particulars to generals). The latter, typically involving predictions, is problematic because there is no *logical* reason (nor empirical data, because an unperceived future event is involved) to justify such claims: that the sun has always risen in the past imposes no logical necessity that it rise tomorrow—we merely assume regularity about the facts involved (see "Hume's Constant Conjunction").

However, Goodman points out, deductive claims are considered valid as long as they correctly follow the rules (that is, it doesn't matter whether or not the conclusion is in accord with the facts—truth is required for soundness, not for validity). So, he asks, what rules would justify inductive claims? "That a given piece of copper conducts electricity increases the credibility of statements asserting that other pieces of copper conduct electricity, and thus confirms the hypothesis that all copper conducts electricity," Goodman notes. "But," he continues, "the fact that a given man now in this room is a third son does not increase the credibility of statements asserting that other men now in this room are third sons, and so does not confirm the hypothesis that all men now in this room are third sons" (73). He therefore suggests that only inductive claims that are *lawlike* statements (such as "Copper conducts electricity") can be confirmed by (particular) past instances.

However, as his thought experiment about "grue" shows, past instances may confirm two incompatible statements: before time *t,* each emerald we find is green and grue, particulars which confirm equally well the general statements that "Emeralds are green" and "Emeralds are grue"; but since after time *t,* all grue emeralds are blue, we seem to have confirmed both "All emeralds are green" and "All emeralds are blue." What went wrong?

Goodman's response is that a definition of "lawlike" is needed—"All emeralds are grue" is apparently *not* a lawlike statement. So for what sorts of statements *is* it valid to reason from particular instances to general claims—that is, what *is* a "lawlike" statement? (What is it—if anything—about the statement "All emeralds are grue" that makes it problematic?)

PLATO'S RING OF GYGES

The story is that [Gyges] was a shepherd in the service of the ruler of Lydia. There was a violent rainstorm and an earthquake which broke open the ground and created a chasm at the place where he was tending sheep. Seeing this and marvelling, he went down into it. He saw . . . a corpse which seemed of more than human stature, wearing nothing but a ring of gold on its finger. This ring the shepherd put on and came out. . . . As he was sitting among the others he happened to twist the hoop of the ring towards himself, to the inside of his hand, and as he did this he became invisible to those sitting near him and they went on talking as if he had gone. He marvelled at this and, fingering the ring, he turned the hoop outward again and became visible. Perceiving this he tested whether the ring had this power and so it happened: if he turned the hoop inwards he became invisible, but was visible when he turned it outwards. When he realized this, he at once arranged to become one of the messengers to the king. He went, committed adultery with the king's wife, attacked the king with her help, killed him, and took over the kingdom.

Now if there were two such rings, one worn by the just man, the other by the unjust, no one, as these people think, would be so incorruptible that he would stay on the path of justice or bring himself to keep away from other people's property and not touch it, when he could with impunity take whatever he wanted from the market, go into houses and have sexual relations with anyone he wanted, kill anyone, free all those he wished from prison, and do the other things which would make him like a god among men. His actions would be in no way different from those of the other and they would both follow the same path.

Source: Plato. *The Republic,* Book II. 380–370 BCE. G. M. A. Grube, trans. Indianapolis: Hackett, 1974. As reprinted in *Moral Philosophy: Selected Readings.* George Sher, ed. San Diego: Harcourt Brace Jovanovich, 1987. 235–243. 237.

This thought experiment is part of a larger discussion about justice and the value of being just (why should we do the right thing?), part of a larger discussion still about what kind of society, and what kind of government, is best. Responding to the claim that success in this world comes to those who are *un*just, Plato's character "Socrates" (who speaks for Plato himself) says that injustice leads to hatred and fighting, while justice results in harmony and a working together of the various parts—both within society as a whole and within the individual.

"Glaucon" then asks Socrates to imagine the scenario he has described. That the just man, if invisible, would act as badly as the unjust man proves, says Glaucon (who is assuming people will do what they believe to be in their own best interest unless compelled otherwise), that being just is *not* in our own best interest: "Every man believes that injustice is much more profitable to himself than justice" (237).

But *would* all of us do whatever we wanted if we knew we wouldn't be caught? If so, does that prove that being good is not good for us? (In which case, why *should* we do the right thing?) Or does it just prove that we don't know, or don't act according to, what's good for us?

GODWIN'S FENELON

In a loose and general view, I and my neighbour are both of us men; and of consequence entitled to equal attention. But in reality, it is probable that one of us is a being of more worth and importance than the other. A man is of more worth than a beast because, being possessed of higher faculties, he is capable of a more refined and genuine happiness. In the same manner, the illustrious archbishop of Cambray [Fenelon] was of more worth than his valet, and there are few of us that would hesitate to pronounce, if his palace were in flames, and the life of only one of them could be preserved, which of the two ought to be preferred.

But there is another ground of preference. . . . We are not connected with one or two percipient beings, but with a society, a nation, and in some sense with the whole family of mankind. Of consequence, that life ought to be preferred which will be most conducive to the general good. In saving the life of Fenelon, suppose at the moment he conceived the project of his immortal *Telemachus,* I [would] have been promoting the benefit of thousands, who have been cured by the perusal of that work, of some error, vice and consequent unhappiness. Nay, my benefit would extend further than this; for every individual, thus cured, has become a better member of society, and has contributed in his turn to the happiness, information and improvement of others.

Suppose I had been myself the valet. . . .

Suppose the valet had been my brother, my father, or my benefactor. . . .

Source: William Godwin. *Enquiry Concerning Political Justice.* 1798. As edited by K. Codell Carter. London: Oxford University Press, 1971. 70–71.

There are several points Godwin makes with this thought experiment. The first is that some people are more valuable than others on intrinsic grounds, because of their greater inherent capacity for "refined and genuine happiness" (70). This opinion is contrary to that of his contemporary Jeremy Bentham, who says, basically, that pinball's as good as poetry (*Introduction to the Principles of Morals and Legislation*, 1789); J. S. Mill, however, differs (agreeing with Godwin) when he says it's better to be a Socrates, even if dissatisfied, than a pig satisfied (*Utilitarianism*, 1861). *Is* it? By what standards do we judge one person's happiness to be worth more than another's? And how could we possibly make such a measurement? Maybe the satisfied pig is really *really* satisfied. Maybe so, Mill might concede, but he claims that anyone who has known both lower (for example, sensory) and higher (for example, intellectual) pleasures would choose the higher. (But has any human being really *known* the pleasures of a pig—a really satisfied pig? See "Nagel's Bat.")

Godwin's second point is that some people (for example, Fenelon) are more valuable than others on instrumental grounds, because of their contribution to "the general good" (70). But can we be sure (and how can we be sure) that Fenelon will make the greater contribution to the happiness of others? And do moral rules determined by consideration of the greatest general good lead to individual well-being (as utilitarianism suggests)?

Godwin's third point addresses the moral permissibility of favoritism (see "Donaldson's Equim"). He claims that Fenelon's life should be chosen over that of himself or one of his relatives because, still, it is more valuable: despite the gratitude or affection he may feel, "justice, pure, unadulterated justice, would still have preferred that which was most valuable" (71). But why is justice more important than gratitude and affection?

MOORE'S TWO WORLDS

Let us imagine one world exceedingly beautiful. Imagine it as beautiful as you can; put into it whatever on this earth you most admire—mountains, rivers, the sea; trees, and sunsets, stars, and moon. Imagine these all combined in the most exquisite proportions, so that no one thing jars against another, but each contributes to increase the beauty of the whole. And then imagine the ugliest world you can possibly conceive. Imagine it simply one heap of filth, containing everything that is most disgusting to us, for whatever reason, and the whole, as far as may be, without one redeeming feature. . . . [No one] ever has or ever, by any possibility, *can,* live in either, can ever see and enjoy the beauty of the one or hate the foulness of the other. . . . [E]ven so, supposing them quite apart from any possible contemplation by human beings, . . . is it irrational to hold that it is better that the beautiful world should exist than the one which is ugly? Would it not be well, in any case, to do what we could to produce it rather than the other?

Source: G. E. Moore. *Principia Ethica.* 1903. Cambridge, UK: Cambridge University Press, 1959. 83–84.

M oore postulates his two worlds in order to challenge the claim that things are good only in relation to human existence. If, as Moore suggests, the beautiful world he describes must be considered a greater good than the ugly world—despite the fact that neither world will be seen by anyone—then "we shall have to include in our ultimate end something beyond the limits of human existence" (84). (Such as?) By implication, hedonism, the view that (human) happiness or pleasure is the sole good, must be rejected.

A criticism of Moore's thought experiment is that it is logically impossible: if the beautiful world is indeed beautiful, it must have been seen by someone, if only an imaginary someone—otherwise, how can it be called beautiful? In other words, the concept of beauty necessarily entails, because it is defined by, human presence. (Must hedonism, therefore, be accepted?)

SMART'S DELUDED SADIST

$\left[\mathbf{L}\right]$et us imagine a universe consisting of one sentient being only, who falsely believes that there are other sentient beings and that they are undergoing exquisite torment. So far from being distressed by the thought, he takes a great delight in these imagined sufferings. Is this better or worse than a universe containing no sentient being at all? Is it worse, again, than a universe containing only one sentient being with the same beliefs as before but who sorrows at the imagined tortures of his fellow creatures?

Source: J. J. C. Smart, *An Outline of a System of Utilitarian Ethics.* Melbourne: Melbourne University Press and Cambridge, UK: Cambridge University Press, 1961. 16.

Smart says the universe with the deluded sadist is the preferable one. His thought experiment therefore shows that pleasure is *intrinsically* good (good in and of itself): "Pleasures are bad," Smart says, "only because they cause harm to the person who has them or to other people" (17)—and, as the sadist *is* deluded, no one *is* being harmed. So if a real person derives pleasure from torturing real people, must one say that *insofar as only the torturer's experience is concerned,* his or her pleasure is a good thing?

If not, then what *is* good—what, other than pleasure, shall we say is intrinsically good? Or shall we say there is *no* intrinsic good? That is, perhaps things are good only *instrumentally,* only according to the effects they bring about. (See "Moore's Two Worlds.") But then how will we determine which effects are good—if not by pleasure, by what?

FOOT'S GAS

Suppose, for instance, that there are five patients in a hospital whose lives could be saved by the manufacture of a certain gas, but that this inevitably releases lethal fumes into the room of another patient whom for some reason we are unable to move.

Is it morally permissible to manufacture the gas?

Source: Philippa Foot. "The Problem of Abortion and the Doctrine of the Double Effect." *Oxford Review* 5 (1967): 5–15. 13.

With this thought experiment, Foot intends to demonstrate that in ethical decisions, the distinction between the positive duty to provide help and the greater negative duty to refrain from injuring is more important than the distinction between intended and unintended effects. The latter distinction is a crucial part of what's called the "doctrine of double effect," which is advocated by adherents of the Roman Catholic religion and especially applicable to decisions about abortion. This doctrine distinguishes between two effects—the intended means and ends of one's actions, and the unintended but foreseeable consequences of one's actions—and evaluates the moral permissibility of an action according to the former rather than the latter. Thus it would be morally permissible for a surgeon to perform a hysterectomy on a pregnant woman; the consequent death of the fetus is merely the unintended but foreseeable consequence of the intended action. Many criticize the doctrine as mere wordplay, pointing out that much depends on how you describe your intent (are you intending to "save the mother" or "kill the fetus"?).

With regard to the scenario Foot describes, according to the doctrine of double effect, it would be morally permissible to manufacture the gas and save the lives of the five—the death of the other person is an unintended side-effect. But this seems wrong, Foot claims. An analysis using positive and negative duties reveals the conflict to be between a positive duty (help the five) and a negative duty (don't harm the other one), and since we are more morally bound to refrain from injury than we are to provide help (negative duties are "stronger" than positive duties), our decision must be, as one would intuitively expect, *not* to manufacture the gas.

But is accordance with our intuition a good test for ethical decision–making approaches? That is, just because the duties approach gives us the answer we intuitively expect, is that a good reason to prefer it? (And *does* our "intuition" tell us, as Foot suggests, *not* to manufacture the gas?)

BRANDT'S SPELUNKERS

Consider . . . a party of spelunkers [cave explorers] by the oceanside. It is found that a rising tide is bringing water into the cave and all will be drowned unless they escape at once. Unfortunately, the first man to try to squeeze through the exit is fat and gets wedged inextricably in the opening, with his head inside the cave. Somebody in the party has a stick of dynamite. Either they blast the fat man out, killing him, or all of them, including him, will drown.

What should the cavers do?

Source: Richard Brandt. "A Moral Principle About Killing." In *Beneficent Euthanasia.* Marvin Kohl, ed. Buffalo, NY: Prometheus Books, 1972. 106–114. 108.

Brandt presents this thought experiment in order to illustrate what he considers to be a deficiency of the view that it is morally wrong to kill innocent human beings. According to that view, Brandt says, all the cavers must drown. Brandt presents an alternative moral principle, one that involves comparing competing moral obligations: one has an obligation not to kill (innocent) human beings *unless* there is a stronger obligation to do something that can't be done without killing. Accordingly, if the cavers' moral obligation to save themselves is stronger than their moral obligation not to kill the one who's stuck, and if saving themselves can't be done *without* killing him, then it is morally permissible for them to do so. (See "Jamieson and Regan's Terrorist Tank.") *Is* their obligation to save themselves stronger than their obligation not to kill him? If so, on what grounds?

As an example of rule utilitarianism (acting in accord with a general rule that will provide the greatest good for the greatest number), Brandt's principle may be criticized for condoning the violation of individual rights—in this case, the right to life. Such critics would choose *not* to blow up the stuck caver because an individual's right to life overrides the greater good. However, Brandt might respond, if you don't blow up the caver, the right to life of *several* people, rather than just of *one,* is violated—and surely that's worse (assuming that each death counts equally or, similarly, that each person has an equal right to life).

Brandt's principle, and utilitarian decisions in general, may also be criticized because certain virtues such as justice and charity are ignored. Blowing up the stuck caver is, after all, neither fair nor charitable. What response might be offered to this criticism?

WILLIAMS'S JIM IN SOUTH AMERICA

Jim finds himself in the central square of a small South American town. Tied up against the wall are a row of twenty Indians, most terrified, a few defiant, in front of them several armed men in uniform. A heavy man in a sweat-stained khaki shirt turns out to be the captain in charge and, after a good deal of questioning of Jim which establishes that he got there by accident while on a botanical expedition, explains that the Indians are a random group of the inhabitants who, after recent acts of protest against the government, are just about to be killed to remind other possible protestors of the advantages of not protesting. However, since Jim is an honoured visitor from another land, the captain is happy to offer him a guest's privilege of killing one of the Indians himself. If Jim accepts, then as a special mark of the occasion, the other Indians will be let off. Of course, if Jim refuses, then there is no special occasion, and Pedro here will do what he was about to do when Jim arrived, and kill them all. Jim, with some desperate recollection of schoolboy fiction, wonders whether if he got hold of a gun, he could hold the captain, Pedro and the rest of the soldiers to threat, but it is quite clear from the set-up that nothing of that kind is going to work: any attempt at that sort of thing will mean that all the Indians will be killed, and himself. The men against the wall, and the other villagers, understand the situation, and are obviously begging him to accept. What should he do?

Source: Bernard Williams. "A Critique of Utilitarianism." In *Utilitarianism: For and Against.* J. J. C. Smart and Bernard Williams, eds. Cambridge, UK: Cambridge University Press, 1973. 77–149. 98–99.

With this scenario, Williams tests the adequacy of utilitarianism. By considering only the consequences (one death is better than twenty deaths and therefore Jim should kill the villager), utilitarianism ignores, Williams says, the notion that we are responsible for what we ourselves do (and not for what others do). Utilitarianism is concerned only with whether X or Y is better; it is indifferent, he says, to *who* does X or Y. However, since the consequence of Jim's refusal is that Pedro will kill twenty people, couldn't one say that Jim is *responsible* for Pedro killing twenty people? No, Williams would reply: Jim, by his refusal, does not *make* Pedro kill twenty people; Pedro is responsible for what he himself does. Does Jim then bear *no* responsibility for the deaths of the villagers?

Nozick's Experience Machine

Suppose there were an experience machine that would give you any experience you desired. Superduper neuropsychologists could stimulate your brain so that you would think and feel you were writing a great novel, or making a friend, or reading an interesting book. All the time you would be floating in a tank, with electrodes attached to your brain. . . . If you are worried about missing out on desirable experiences, we can suppose that business enterprises have researched thoroughly the lives of many others. You can pick and choose from their large library or smorgasbord of such experiences, selecting your life's experiences for, say, the next two years. After two years have passed, you will have ten minutes or ten hours out of the tank, to select the experiences of your *next* two years. Of course, while in the tank you won't know that you're there; you'll think it's all actually happening. . . . Would you plug in?

Source: Robert Nozick. *Anarchy, State, and Utopia.* New York: Basic Books, 1974. 42–43.

The question Nozick is asking is "What else can matter to us, other than how our lives feel from the inside?" (43). Nozick considers three possible answers. Perhaps what matters is the desire to do, rather than just experience, certain things; the experience machine doesn't seem to allow those desires. (But what if the machine could—what if it could enable not only the experience but also the desire for the experience?) Or perhaps what matters is the desire to be a certain sort of person; a blob in the experience machine tank can't be said to be, for example, courageous, kind, intelligent, witty, or loving (43). (Well, suggests Nozick, "imagine a transformation machine which transforms us into whatever sort of person we'd like to be" [44].) Or perhaps what matters is the possibility of some sort of transcendent experience; the experience machine is limited to providing only experiences conceived by humans. Nozick concludes that we would *not* plug in because "what we desire is to live (an active verb) ourselves, in contact with reality" (45).

Nozick's thought experiment is part of a larger discussion about the moral limits to what we may do to each other. With it, he questions the hedonistic view (which considers only one's experiences, one's pleasure and pain, in determining such limits) and the derivative utilitarian view (which advocates that we should do that which promotes the greatest good, measured in terms of pleasure, for the greatest number). Since something besides our experience (of pleasure) matters to us, Nozick suggests that something else should be considered when determining what actions are morally permissible. (What might this "something else" be?)

FEINBERG'S EGOIST

Imagine a person (let's call him "Jones") who is, first of all, devoid of intellectual curiosity. He has no desire to acquire any kind of knowledge for its own sake, and thus is utterly indifferent to questions of science, mathematics, and philosophy. Imagine further that the beauties of nature leave Jones cold: he is unimpressed by the autumn foliage, the snow-capped mountains, and the rolling oceans. Long walks in the country on spring mornings and skiing forays in the winter are to him equally a bore. Moreover, let us suppose that Jones can find no appeal in art. Novels are dull, poetry a pain, paintings nonsense, and music just noise. Suppose further that Jones has neither the participant's nor the spectator's passion for baseball, football, tennis, or any other sport. Swimming to him is a cruel aquatic form of calisthenics, the sun only a cause of sunburn. Dancing is coeducational idiocy, conversation a waste of time, the other sex an unappealing mystery. Politics is a fraud, religion mere superstition; and the misery of millions of underprivileged human beings is nothing to be concerned with or excited about. Suppose finally that Jones has no talent for any kind of handicraft, industry, or commerce, and that he does not regret that fact.

What then is Jones interested in? He must desire something. To be sure, he does. Jones has an overwhelming passion for, a complete preoccupation with, his own happiness. The one exclusive desire of his life is *to be happy*.

Will Jones be able to satisfy his desire to be happy?

Source: Joel Feinberg. "Psychological Egoism." In *Reason and Responsibility: Readings in Some Basic Problems of Philosophy.* 3rd ed. Joel Feinberg, ed. Encino, CA: Dickenson, 1975. 501–512. 505.

"Psychological egoism" is a theory that maintains that we are motivated, only and always, by our own self-interest, by our desire for our own happiness, and that, therefore, we are incapable of purely altruistic desires and acts. Philosophers are interested in psychological egoism because if it is indeed true, then many theories about what we *should* do are useless—for what's the point in saying we *should* do *X* if we *can't* do *X* (because we can only do *Y*)? (That is, "ought" should imply "can"—the "ought implies can" principle.) More specifically, if psychological egoism is true (we act according to our own self-interest), then virtue ethics (we should act in accordance to certain virtues such as honesty and generosity), utilitarian ethics (we should act so as to bring about the greatest good for the greatest number), and so on are merely interesting intellectual exercises and not valuable prescriptions for morally acceptable human behavior.

Feinberg presents this thought experiment in order to demonstrate that psychological egoism is untenable, for Feinberg claims that Jones will not be able to satisfy his desire to be happy. People can be happy, Feinberg claims, only when they desire something *other than* their own happiness. And since many people *are* happy, it follows that many people *do* desire something other than their own happiness. Therefore, psychological egoism is false.

Is Feinberg's claim true? *Can* we be happy only when we desire something other than our own happiness? *Is* Jones destined to a life of unhappiness because, paradoxically, his only desire is for happiness? What if Smith, let us suppose, does desire knowledge, nature, art, sports, and so on—but *only because* such things make her happy? If indeed she is able to be happy, would that not support psychological egoism—and defeat Feinberg's claim?

JAMIESON AND REGAN'S CHAINSAW

Imagine you have borrowed a chainsaw from a friend, promising to return it whenever he asks for it. Imagine he turns up at your door in a visibly drunken state, accompanied by a bound and gagged companion who has already been severely beaten and is in a state of terror. "I'll have my chainsaw now," he intones. Ought you to return it, under those circumstances?

Source: Dale Jamieson and Tom Regan. "On the Ethics of the Use of Animals in Science." In *And Justice for All: New Introductory Essays in Ethics and Public Policy.* Tom Regan and Donald Van De Veer, eds. Totowa, NJ: Rowman & Allanheld, 1982. 169–196. 179.

J amieson and Regan use this scenario[1] in order to explore the implications of moral absolutes. Their response is that one ought *not* fetch the chainsaw. However, they claim, admitting exceptions to a moral rule does not mean the rule is taken any less seriously. It simply means that there are other considerations that bear on the morality of what one ought to do; in this case, the likely consequences should be considered in addition to one's having made a promise. One might ask, though, *when* do the consequences override the promise? And are *all* moral absolutes subject to being overridden by consequences?

This scenario (and others like it, of course) can also be approached as a conflict between competing values: in this case, one must choose between keeping a promise and preventing a harm; whatever one does will be "wrong," so one must choose, as it were, "the lesser of two evils." (And how does one determine which is the lesser of two evils?)

---

[1] It's reminiscent of Plato's "Suppose that a friend when in his right mind has deposited arms with me and he asks for them when he is not in his right mind; ought I to give them back to him?" (*Republic,* Book I)—but this rendition is much funnier.

JAMIESON AND REGAN'S
TERRORIST TANK

Imagine that a terrorist has possession of a well-armed tank and is systematically slaughtering forty-five innocent hostages whom he has fastened to a wall. Attempts to negotiate a compromise fail. The man will kill all the hostages if we do nothing. Under the circumstances, there is only one reasonable alternative: blow up the tank. But there is this complication: the terrorist has strapped a young girl to the tank, and any weapon sufficient to blow up the tank will kill the child. The girl is innocent. Thus to blow up the tank is to harm an innocent, one who herself stands no chance of benefiting from the attack. Ought we to blow up the tank?

Source: Dale Jamieson and Tom Regan. "On the Ethics of the Use of Animals in Science." In *And Justice for All: New Introductory Essays in Ethics and Public Policy.* Tom Regan and Donald Van De Veer, eds. Totowa, NJ: Rowman & Allanheld, 1982. 169–196. 180.

Jamieson and Regan use this scenario[1] in order to explore the circumstances under which it is morally permissible to harm innocent people (having rejected the view that such a moral principle is absolute). They suggest that "it is wrong to harm an innocent individual unless it is reasonable to believe that doing so is the only realistic way of avoiding equal harm for many other innocents" (180) and, accordingly, conclude that it would be morally permissible to blow up the tank. (See "Brandt's Spelunkers.")

They concede that defining "equal harm" will be difficult: "It is a matter of degree how much a given harm will detract from an individual's well-being, and problems will arise concerning just how serious a given harm is, or whether two or more different harms are 'equal'" (180). What criteria might be used to measure harm? Deciding how many other innocents is "many" will also be difficult—"If the only way to avoid the death of two innocents is to kill one, ought we to do this?" (180). What if the death of not two, but two hundred, or two million, is avoided by killing one?

---

[1]They developed it from a reference by Robert Nozick (in *Anarchy, State and Utopia*) to "innocent persons strapped onto the front of the tanks of aggressors" (35) as an example of *innocent shields of threats,* presented by Nozick as a complication of *innocent threats:* "If someone picks up a third party and throws him at you down at the bottom of a deep well, the third party is innocent and a threat; had he chosen to launch himself at you in that trajectory he would be an aggressor. Even though the falling person would survive his fall onto you, may you use your ray gun to disintegrate the falling body before it crushes and kills you?" (34). Nozick argues that while a principle of nonaggression may prohibit using violence against an *innocent person,* a different principle may be required for innocent shields of threats (such as the person strapped to the tank) and innocent threats (such as the third party thrown down the well). He then asks, "*If* one may attack an aggressor and injure an innocent shield, may the innocent shield fight back in self-defense (supposing that he cannot move against or fight the aggressor)? Do we get two persons battling each other in self-defense? Similarly, if you use force against an innocent threat to you, do you thereby become an innocent threat to him, so that he may justifiably use additional force against you (supposing that he can do this, yet cannot prevent his original threateningness)?" (35).

THOMSON'S TROLLEY PROBLEM

Suppose you are the driver of a trolley. The trolley rounds a bend, and there come into view ahead five track workmen, who have been repairing the track. The track goes through a bit of a valley at that point, and the sides are steep, so you must stop the trolley if you are to avoid running the five men down. You step on the brakes, but alas they don't work. Now you suddenly see a spur of track leading off to the right. You can turn the trolley onto it, and thus save the five men on the straight track ahead. Unfortunately, . . . there is one track workman on that spur of track. He can no more get off the track in time than the five can, so you will kill him if you turn the trolley onto him. Is it morally permissible for you to turn the trolley?

Source: Judith Jarvis Thomson. "The Trolley Problem." *Yale Law Journal* 94 (1985): 1395–1415. 1395.

According to Philippa Foot, who initially posed the trolley problem, the choice is between killing one person and killing five people; the situation is one of competing negative duties (see "Foot's Gas"), specifically the duty to refrain from injuring or killing others, and one should choose the lesser violation.

However, Thomson, who extensively discusses and develops the trolley problem, disagrees with that description: Imagine, she says, that Frank is a passenger on the trolley and the driver has just died of shock upon discovering that the brakes have failed; if Frank chooses not to turn the trolley, he can hardly be said to kill five people since, in that case, he wouldn't have *done* anything. So the choice is between killing one person and letting five die. While Thomson agrees that someone may turn the trolley and thereby kill the one person, she notes that this challenges the commonly held opinion that killing is worse than letting die. (See "Rachels's Smith and Jones at the Bathtub.")

Furthermore, Thomson continues, one must consider the circumstances. For example, do the six people have equal claims against the trolley? Since this is an odd sort of question, she suggests that we imagine another situation: "Suppose there are six men who are dying. Five are standing in one clump on the beach, one is standing further along. Floating in on the tide is a marvelous pebble, the Health-pebble . . . it cures what ails you. The one needs for cure the whole Health-Pebble; each of the five needs only a fifth of it. Now in fact that Health-Pebble is drifting towards the one, so that if nothing is done to alter its course, the one will get it. We happen to be swimming nearby, and are in a position to deflect it towards the five" (209).[1] If and only if all six people have an equal claim to the pebble, Thomson says, may we deflect it from the one to the five; we may not do so if the one owns the pebble, for example. Similarly, Thomson asks, what if all six people on the trolley track have been informed of the risk, are paid well to assume that risk, and have drawn straws for their work positions that day? Alternatively, what if the one is a convalescent from a nearby hospital who is having lunch on a picnic table put on the trolley track by the mayor who has informed everyone the track is no longer used and is a perfectly safe place for a picnic (and who is, by the way, Frank, the passenger on the trolley)? Are there criteria other than claims to be considered? (How about intrinsic and instrumental worth? See "Godwin's Fenelon.")

[1]Judith Jarvis Thomson. "Killing, Letting Die, and the Trolley Problem." *The Monist* 59 (1976): 204–217.

Thomson's Transplant Problem

[I]magine yourself to be a surgeon, a truly great surgeon. Among other things you do, you transplant organs, and you are such a great surgeon that the organs you transplant always take. At the moment, you have five patients who need organs. Two need one lung each, two need a kidney each, and the fifth needs a heart. If they do not get those organs today, they will all die; if you find organs for them today, you can transplant the organs and they will all live. But where to find the lungs, the kidneys, and the heart? The time is almost up when a report is brought to you that a young man who has just come into your clinic for his yearly check-up has exactly the right blood-type and is in excellent health. Lo, you have a possible donor. All you need do is cut him up and distribute *his* parts among the five who need them. You ask, but he says, "Sorry. I deeply sympathize, but no." Would it be morally permissible for you to operate anyway?

Source: Judith Jarvis Thomson. "The Trolley Problem." *Yale Law Journal* 94 (1985): 1395–1415. 1396.

Thomson expects us to say "no" and asks then why is it morally permissible for the trolley driver to turn the trolley and thus save the five (see "Thomson's Trolley Problem") but not morally permissible for the surgeon to operate and thus save the five? A reasonable response, suggests Thomson, is to appeal to the Kantian notion that it is wrong to use a person as a means only.[1] Clearly the surgeon would be using the one person as a means to save the five. In particular, the surgeon would be using the person's body parts, to which the person has a special right or claim. And such rights or claims of the one "trump" the general good of the five. (*Do* they?) (See "Brandt's Spelunkers.") Since this is not the case in the trolley problem, one may go ahead and turn the trolley toward the one. (But suppose, Thomson says, you are on a bridge overlooking the trolley track and, since you know trolleys, you know the one approaching is out of control and the only way to save the five people on the track is to push a large person off the bridge onto the path of the trolley, which will, as a result, come to a stop; or suppose the diverging track forms a closed loop instead of a fork, and when you switch to take the track leading to the one person, it is *by* hitting that one person, which causes the trolley to stop, that you save the five.)

Furthermore, suggests Thomson, another difference that might explain why the surgeon may not operate but the trolley driver may turn the trolley is that in the trolley problem, the driver deflects a preexisting and inevitable threat (the runaway trolley) from a larger group (the five people) onto a smaller one (the one person); however, in the transplant case, the surgeon poses a new, different threat to the smaller group (being cut up for parts wouldn't have otherwise happened). (But the one person would've died anyway, otherwise, eventually. . . .)

---

[1] And yet consider C. D. Broad's scenario (*Five Types of Ethical Theory*, 1967) in which a man who is a carrier of typhoid is isolated: "We are *pro tanto* treating him merely as a cause of infection to others. But, if we refuse to isolate him, we are treating other people *pro tanto* merely as means to his comfort and culture" (132). This shows, Broad says, that it is sometimes impossible to adhere to Kant's moral rule to treat people never as a means to an end but always as ends in themselves. In the situation Broad describes, both actions—isolating the man and not isolating him—will violate Kant's moral rule.

DONALDSON'S EQUIM

Consider a hypothetical world in which impartiality is a dominant norm. This world, known as Equim, is inhabited by persons [whose] natural desires do not foster moral partiality of any sort. . . . [People in Equim] are equally fond of everyone. . . .

. . . [They] do not have friends as such since all persons are equal objects of concern and respect. In Equim, a person confronted with the tragic choice of saving his own child or that of a stranger would attempt to ensure the impartiality of his choice; indeed, time allowing, she would make use of a random generating procedures such as flipping a coin. . . .

. . . Families, nations, and social clubs are either non-existent or arranged only for purposes of efficiency. . . .

. . . [T]he overall amount of happiness in Equim is slightly greater than in the present world. Assume this is true not only for the society as a whole, but for each individual person. . . .

Suppose you could take a pill and have the same rearranged constitution of desires as people in Equim. Would you? *Should* you?

Source: Thomas Donaldson. "Morally Privileged Relationships." *Journal of Value Inquiry* 24 (1990): 1–15. 4–5. Copyright © Kluwer Academic Publishers. Reprinted by permission of Kluwer Academic Publishers and the author.

Donaldson's Equim is part of an investigation into the question "Can favoritism be morally justified?" He anticipates that most people would prefer our world to that of Equim: "A world of no friendship and of no neighborly or family affection is one few would choose to inhabit even on the condition that it yielded slight gains in overall happiness" (5). No doubt, he's correct—most of us would not choose to live in Equim.

But shouldn't we? Isn't the greater happiness in Equim preferable? And isn't the justice of impartiality preferable? In fact, isn't our "natural" partiality, or preference for particular individuals, just a matter of accident? While we may "choose" our friends, at least from the "available" options, we surely don't choose our family members. Is such "accident" a sound basis for morality?

One argument to justify favoritism appeals to "promises, socially structured duties, and contracts" (3); thus, for example, one is morally "allowed" to "favor" someone to whom one has made a promise or with whom one has made a contract. But why make promises to those particular people—how do you justify the *initial* partiality? Perhaps an answer is provided by another argument that appeals to the "social good" consequences of certain loyalties and institutions such as friendships and families; thus, for example, one is morally allowed to favor one's own children over others' children. But, as Donaldson suggests with Equim (is he correct?), a world without such loyalties and institutions would result in *greater* social good. (See "Godwin's Fenelon.") So how can the partiality we seem to prefer be morally justified?

Thomson's Violinist

[L]et me ask you to imagine this. You wake up in the morning and find yourself back to back in bed with an unconscious violinist. A famous unconscious violinist. He has been found to have a fatal kidney ailment, and the Society of Music Lovers has canvassed all the available medical records and found that you alone have the right blood type to help. They have therefore kidnapped you, and last night the violinist's circulatory system was plugged into yours, so that your kidneys can be used to extract poisons from his blood as well as your own. The director of the hospital now tells you, "Look, we're sorry the Society of Music Lovers did this to you—we would never have permitted it if we had known. But still, they did it, and the violinist now is plugged into you. To unplug you would be to kill him. But never mind, it's only for nine months. By then he will have recovered from his ailment, and can safely be unplugged from you." Is it morally incumbent on you to accede to this situation?

Source: Judith Jarvis Thomson. "A Defense of Abortion." *Philosophy & Public Affairs* 1.1 (Fall 1971): 47–66. 48–49.

Thomson proposes this thought experiment in order to explore the ethics of abortion. Specifically, it puts to the test the argument that abortion is wrong because the fetus's right to life overrides the pregnant person's right to decide what happens in and to her body. If we answer Thomson's question with a "no," then, by analogy, we are saying there is something wrong with that argument. (Abortion may be morally wrong on other grounds, but not that one.)

To highlight her point, Thomson asks, "What if it were not nine months, but nine years? Or longer still?" (49). She also asks, "What if it were just one hour?" (59). If we modify our answer according to the time involved, Thomson suggests, we are saying that whether one has a right to something depends on how easy or convenient it is to get that something—and surely that can't be the case. (At this point, it might be helpful to note Thomson's distinction between something being "nice" or "generous" and something being "morally required"—it might be generous, and morally *good*, if the person went along with the situation, but he or she may not be morally *required* to do so.)

Note that in the scenario Thomson describes, the person was kidnapped and connected to the violinist against his or her will—he or she did not want the situation to occur. This is intended to parallel unwanted pregnancy. Would our response be different if the person had agreed? (And does agreeing to sexual intercourse mean you're agreeing to pregnancy? What about sexual intercourse with correctly and carefully used contraception? See "Thomson's People-seeds.") If our response *would* be different, then we are saying that sometimes a fetus *has* the right to use a woman's body (and so abortion is morally wrong) and sometimes it *doesn't* (so abortion is morally acceptable). Do we really want to say that the fetus's right to life depends on how that life came to be? That is, fetuses that come into existence as a result of rape don't have a right to life, or have less of a right to life than those that come into existence as a result of consensual sex? (Alternatively, perhaps then it's not the fetus's right to life that is affected by whether or not it was intended, but the woman's right to decide what happens in and to her body.)

Furthermore, what exactly does "right to life" mean? Thomson argues that "needing X to live" doesn't necessarily lead to "having a right to X"— the violinist needs your kidneys to live, but does that mean he has a right to them? If not, when—if ever—*would* he have a right to them? (When *does* something have a right to life?)

THOMSON'S GROWING
CHILD IN A TINY HOUSE

Suppose you find yourself trapped in a tiny house with a growing child. I mean a very tiny house, and a rapidly growing child—you are already up against the wall of the house and in a few minutes you'll be crushed to death. The child on the other hand won't be crushed to death; if nothing is done to stop him from growing he'll be hurt, but in the end he'll simply burst open the house and walk out a free man.

Is it morally permissible to stop the child from growing?

Source: Judith Jarvis Thomson. "A Defense of Abortion." *Philosophy & Public Affairs* 1.1 (Fall 1971): 47–66. 52.

Thomson's response is that while a bystander may not choose between your life and the child's life and so may not intervene, surely you yourself are not morally required to wait passively until you are crushed to death—surely you are morally permitted to defend or save yourself even if that means the child dies. Because the scenario is intended to parallel pregnancy, Thomson is arguing that abortion is morally permissible on the grounds of self-defense. "Perhaps a pregnant woman is vaguely felt to have the status of [a] house, to which we don't allow the right of self-defense," she adds, "[b]ut if the woman houses the child, it should be remembered that she is a *person* who houses it" (52–53 emphasis added).

So would Thomson's argument apply only to pregnancies that threaten the life of the pregnant person? And even in those cases, is the right to self-defense unlimited? (See "Thomson's People-seeds.") Lastly, does Thomson's argument permit only abortions that are literally do-it-yourself?

THOMSON'S PEOPLE-SEEDS

[S]uppose it were like this: people-seeds drift about in the air like pollen, and if you open your windows, one may drift in and take root in your carpets or upholstery. You don't want children, so you fix up your windows with fine mesh screens, the very best you can buy. As can happen, however, and on very, very rare occasions does happen, one of the screens is defective; and a seed drifts in and takes root. Does the person-plant who now develops have a right to the use of your house?

Source: Judith Jarvis Thomson. "A Defense of Abortion." *Philosophy & Public Affairs* 1.1 (Fall 1971): 47–66. 59.

This scenario is intended to parallel unwanted conception, and the issue Thomson is exploring is whether or not a fetus can be said to have acquired a right to the use of a person's body. If a fetus *does* acquire such a right, then a woman's right to self-defense, through abortion, is limited. (See "Thomson's Growing Child in a Tiny House.")

Thomson claims that the person-plant does *not* have a right to the use of your house, "despite the fact that you voluntarily opened your windows, you knowingly kept carpets and upholstered furniture, and you knew that screens were sometimes defective" (59); a burglar climbing into your house through an open window, or because of a defect in the bars you had installed across the window, has no right to stay inside and/or use your house. And she dismisses the suggestion that the person-plant *does* have such a right because, after all, "you *could* have lived out your life with bare floors and furniture, or with sealed windows and doors" (59). Consequently, Thomson would argue, you have a right to vacuum.

When *would* a fetus have a right to the use of a person's body? That is, what would you have to do or not do in order for abortion to qualify as a violation of that right? (And would such a violation always make abortion morally unjustified?)

TOOLEY'S KITTEN

Suppose at some future time a chemical were to be discovered which when injected into the brain of a kitten would cause the kitten to develop into a cat possessing a brain of the sort possessed by humans, and consequently into a cat having all the psychological capabilities characteristic of adult humans. Such cats would be able to think, to use language, and so on. Now it would surely be morally indefensible in such a situation to ascribe a serious right to life to members of the species Homo sapiens without also ascribing it to cats that have undergone such a process of development: there would be no morally significant differences.

Secondly, it would not be seriously wrong to refrain from injecting a newborn kitten with the special chemical, and to kill it instead. The fact that one could initiate a causal process that would transform a kitten into an entity that would eventually possess properties such that anything possessing them *ipso facto* has a serious right to life does not mean that the kitten has a serious right to life even before it has been subjected to the process of injection and transformation. . . .

Thirdly, . . . if it is not seriously wrong to refrain from initiating such a causal process, neither is it seriously wrong to interfere with such a process. Suppose a kitten is accidentally injected with the chemical. As long as it has not yet developed those properties that in themselves endow something with a right to life, there cannot be anything wrong with interfering with the causal process and preventing the development of the properties in question. . . .

Source: Michael Tooley. "Abortion and Infanticide." *Philosophy and Public Affairs* 2.1 (1972): 37–65. 60–61. Copyright © 1972 Blackwell Publishers.

Tooley uses this thought experiment to examine the argument against abortion and infanticide that appeals to potential: it is morally wrong to kill adult human beings; embryos, fetuses, and newborns (typically) have the potential to become adult human beings; therefore, it is also morally wrong to kill embryos, fetuses, and newborns. The argument is attractive for two reasons: one need not define exactly what property warrants the right to life (rationality, personhood, or whatever), and one need not define exactly when that property is achieved (at conception, at some point during the pregnancy, or at birth). One need establish only that adult human beings have it and that embryos, fetuses, and newborns have the potential to develop, in the normal course of events, into adult human beings.

Tooley concludes, as a result of his thought experiment, that "if it is not seriously wrong to destroy an injected kitten which will naturally develop the properties that bestow a right to life, neither can it be seriously wrong to destroy a member of *Homo sapiens* which lacks such properties, but will naturally come to have them" (61). *Is* it morally acceptable to destroy an injected kitten? And is an injected kitten similar in relevant ways to an embryo or a fetus?

WARREN'S SPACE TRAVELER

Imagine a space traveler who lands on an unknown planet and encounters a race of beings utterly unlike any he has ever seen or heard of. If he wants to be sure of behaving morally toward these beings, he has to somehow decide whether they are people, and hence have full moral rights, or whether they are the sort of thing which he need not feel guilty about treating as, for example, a source of food.

How should he go about making this decision?

Source: Mary Anne Warren. "On the Moral and Legal Status of Abortion." *The Monist* 57.1 (January 1973): 43–61. 54.

W arren presents this thought experiment in the context of a discussion about the moral permissibility of abortion. Having rejected the view that only *human beings* (that is, those with the human genetic code) have full and equal moral rights (including the right to life), she claims that only *persons* have such rights—hence, her desire to establish the criteria that would qualify one as a person.

The presence of religion, art, tools, or shelter may indicate that the alien beings are people; however, Warren says, the *absence* of such cultural characteristics would not necessarily indicate they are *not* people, since they may have progressed beyond or without those characteristics.

One of the criteria she suggests instead is consciousness. But what exactly is consciousness? And how can we know the aliens are conscious? Other possible criteria are the ability to reason and the capacity to communicate. However, defining and establishing the ability to reason and the capacity to communicate may be as problematic. (What other possibilities are there—what makes something a *person?*)

Furthermore, many of the attributes one might suggest are matters of degree. So how conscious, for example, must the aliens be before we consider them conscious enough to be persons? And would an alien be more of a person, with more rights, the more conscious it is?

Insofar as Warren is concerned with determining whether abortion is morally permissible, since a fetus has none of the traits she mentions (she also suggests self-motivated activity and the presence of self-concepts), it is not a person; therefore, it has no right to life; and abortion is, therefore, morally permissible. One could point out, however, that a newborn has none of the traits mentioned either—does that mean that infanticide is also morally permissible?

WARREN'S SPACE EXPLORER

Suppose that our space explorer falls into the hands of an alien culture, whose scientists decide to create a few hundred thousand or more human beings, by breaking his body into its component cells, and using these to create fully developed human beings, with, of course, his genetic code. We may imagine that each of these newly created men will have all of the original man's abilities, skills, knowledge, and so on, and also have an individual self-concept, in short that each of them will be a bona fide (though hardly unique) person. Imagine that the whole project will take only seconds, and that its chances of success are extremely high, and that our explorer knows all of this, and also knows that these people will be treated fairly. [Would the space explorer have] a right to escape if he could, and thus to deprive all of these potential people of their potential lives[?]

Source: Mary Anne Warren. "On the Moral and Legal Status of Abortion." *The Monist* 57.1 (January 1973): 43–61. 59–60.

W hile there may be something immoral about *wantonly* destroying potential people, Warren says, "the rights of any *actual* person invariably outweigh those of any *potential* person, whenever the two conflict" (59, emphasis added)—so our space explorer *does* have the right to escape. Likewise, Warren argues, pregnant people have the right to abort. (See "Tooley's Kitten.")

Does it matter, though, whether the conflict is between two similar and perhaps "equal" rights (for example, as in Warren's thought experiment, between the potential person's right to life and the actual person's right to life) or between two different and perhaps "unequal" rights (as in questions of abortion, between the potential person's right to life and the actual person's right to be pregnancy free)? Warren anticipates this question and responds, "I think [the space explorer] would have a right to escape even if it were not his life which the alien scientists planned to take, but only a year of his freedom, or, indeed, only a day" (60). (See "Thomson's Violinist.") She goes on, "Nor would he be obligated to stay if he had gotten captured (thus bringing all these people-potentials into existence) because of his own carelessness, or even if he had done so deliberately, knowing the consequences. . . . [O]ne actual person's right to liberty [and, she adds later, the right to protect one's health and happiness] outweighs whatever right to life even a hundred thousand potential people have" (60). What grounds might Warren offer for this claim?

Sylvan's Last People

Let us assume that the last people are very numerous. [And they know they are the last people, e.g. because they are aware that radiation effects have blocked any chance of reproduction.] They humanely exterminate every wild animal and they eliminate the fish of the seas, they put all arable land under intensive cultivation, and all remaining forests disappear in favor of quarries or plantations, and so on. They may give various familiar reasons for this, e.g. they believe it is the way to salvation or to perfection, or they are simply satisfying reasonable needs, or even that it is needed to keep the last people employed or occupied so that they do not worry too much about their impending extinction.

Have they done wrong?

Source: Richard Sylvan (formerly Richard Routley). "Is There a Need for a New, an Environmental, Ethic?" In *Proceedings of the 15th World Congress of Philosophy,* no. 1. Varna, Bulgaria, 1973. As reprinted in *Environmental Philosophy: From Animal Rights to Radical Ecology.* 2nd ed. Michael E. Zimmerman, ed. Upper Saddle River, NJ: Prentice-Hall, 1998. 17–25. 21. Reprinted by permission of the author.

According to the standard view that one may do as one wants as long as one doesn't harm others (or oneself), the last people have *not* done wrong. But, Sylvan suggests, surely they have. (*Have* they?) Therefore, he claims, a new ethic is needed to replace that standard view. What principles should be included in this new ethic? That is, what principles have the last people violated?

One possibility is to say that it is wrong to destroy the natural environment. On what basis? In any case?

Another possibility is to extend the definition of "harm" to include the distress caused to those of the last people who value other (that is, nonhuman) animals, forests, lakes, clear skies, clean rain, and so on. What would the implications be if we were to include such "distress" in our definition of "harm"?

Yet another possibility is to extend the definition of "others." For example, it might include future people (see "The Routleys' Nuclear Train"); however, in this case, there are no future people—these are the last people. It might instead, as Sylvan suggests, include "others who would be so affected [killed or displaced] by the action in question were they placed in the environment" (22–23). He also suggests that "others" include members of other species—not necessarily because they have rights but because we have responsibilities. (Indeed, Sylvan calls the "no harm" principle, as well as the "social contract" principle and the Kantian "treat others as ends only" principle, chauvinistic because such principles put humans first "and everything else a bad last" [20].) What responsibilities might Sylvan have in mind? On what basis might we have these responsibilities? And do we incur these responsibilities only when we become the last people or do we have them now?

RACHELS'S SMITH AND JONES AT THE BATHTUB

[L]et us consider this pair of cases:

In the first, Smith stands to gain a large inheritance if anything should happen to his six-year-old cousin. One evening while the child is taking his bath, Smith sneaks into the bathroom and drowns the child, and then arranges things so that it will look like an accident.

In the second, Jones also stands to gain if anything should happen to his six-year-old cousin. Like Smith, Jones sneaks in planning to drown the child in his bath. However, just as he enters the bathroom Jones sees the child slip and hit his head, and fall face down in the water. Jones is delighted; he stands by, ready to push the child's head back under if it is necessary, but it is not necessary. With only a little thrashing about, the child drowns all by himself, "accidentally," as Jones watches and does nothing.

Now Smith killed the child, whereas Jones "merely" let the child die. That is the only difference between them. Did either man behave better, from a moral point of view?

Source: James Rachels. "Active and Passive Euthanasia." *New England Journal of Medicine* 292.2 (January 9, 1975): 78–80. 79.

This scenario explores the ethics of euthanasia, specifically the moral difference between active euthanasia (taking direct action, such as administering a lethal dose of a drug, which results in a person's death) and passive euthanasia (withholding—stopping or not starting—treatment and thus allowing a person to die). Rachels expects that we will say that Smith and Jones are equally guilty of wrongdoing. He agrees: both Smith and Jones had the same motive (personal gain) and the same intent (to bring about the child's death); that they exhibited different behavior to achieve that end (Smith "did something" by holding the kid under water, whereas Jones "did nothing" by just standing beside the tub) is morally irrelevant. Likewise, Rachels is saying, there is no moral difference between active euthanasia and passive euthanasia. In fact, Rachels goes on to argue, the behavior of *both* Smith and Jones could be described as active—refusing to help is actively staying put, actively holding one's arms to one's sides.

There are differences between Rachels's scenario and euthanasia—in particular, doctors are generally not motivated by personal gain. But Rachels's experiment was set up to test the moral value of active and passive behavior, so he kept constant all the variables of behavior (such as motive and intent) except the crucial one intended for measure (active versus passive). It may be that euthanasia is morally wrong if done for personal gain, but it would be equally wrong whether it were done "actively" or "passively"—that's Rachels's point; likewise, euthanasia done for humane reasons is morally acceptable whether it's done "actively" or "passively." In fact, as Rachels points out, the slow and painful deaths that occur when one is "left to die" provide strong grounds for claiming that passive euthanasia is morally *un*acceptable.

But with active euthanasia, some *person* causes another person's death; with passive euthanasia, some *disease or injury* causes death. Is that not a significant—a *morally* significant—difference? (Is it morally significant only if "causing death" is a bad thing?)

Harris's Survival Lottery

Y and Z put forward the following scheme: they propose that everyone be given a sort of lottery number. Whenever doctors have two or more dying patients [who had not brought their misfortunes on themselves] who could be saved by transplants, and no suitable organs have come to hand through "natural" deaths, they can ask a central computer to supply a suitable donor. The computer will then pick the number of a suitable donor at random and he will be killed so that the lives of two or more others may be saved. No doubt if the scheme were ever to be implemented, a suitable euphemism for "killed" would be employed. Perhaps we would begin to talk about citizens being called upon to "give life" to others. With the refinement of transplant procedures, such a scheme could offer the chance of saving large numbers of lives that are now lost. Indeed, even taking into account the loss of the lives of donors, the numbers of untimely deaths each year might be dramatically reduced, so much so that everyone's chance of living to a ripe old age might be increased. . . .

Suppose that inter-planetary travel revealed a world of people like ourselves, but who organized their society according to this scheme. No one was considered to have an absolute right to life or freedom from interference, but everything was always done to ensure that as many people as possible would enjoy long and happy lives. In such a world a man who attempted to escape when his number was up or who resisted on the grounds that no one had a right to take his life might well be regarded as a murderer. We might or might not prefer to live in such a world, but the morality of its inhabitants would surely be one that we could respect. It would not be obviously more barbaric or cruel or immoral than our own.

Source: John Harris. "The Survival Lottery." *Philosophy* 50 (1975): 81–87. 83. Copyright © The Royal Institute of Philosophy 1975.

One might claim, however, that such a system *would* be immoral because it's wrong to kill the innocent. But suppose the dying patients are no less innocent than the chosen donors: with or without the system, innocents will die, so is it not better that one die instead of two? (See "Thomson's Trolley Problem.")

What about an objection based on self-defense? Doesn't the person selected by the lottery have a right to defend him- or herself against being killed? One can counter that the dying person has a similar right. As Harris points out, "while it is true that they [the dying] can live only if another man is killed, they would claim that it is also true that if they are left to die, then someone who lives on does so over their dead bodies" (85). Of course, being "left to die" isn't the same as being "killed"—is it? (See "Rachels's Smith and Jones at the Bathtub.")

Another possible objection to Harris's lottery system is that we shouldn't interfere with God's plans regarding who lives and who dies. But, one can counter, we already do just that by performing transplants when organs are available through the donor system. (And anyway, there may not be a god. With plans. See "Hume's Infant, Inferior, or Superannuated Deity.")

Yet another objection might be that who lives and who dies shouldn't be "determined" by "the luck of the draw." But, one can counter, again, it already is—those who die are simply those unlucky enough to become terminally ill. (So is our current notion of a right to life actually based on mere chance? That is, you have a right to life only as long as you happen to have a healthy body? If so, it would seem to rest on grounds no stronger than those supporting Harris's survival lottery. . . .)

THE ROUTLEYS' NUCLEAR TRAIN

A long-distance country train has just pulled out. The train, which is crowded, carries both passengers and freight. At an early stop in the journey, someone consigns as freight, to a far distant destination, a package which contains a highly toxic and explosive gas. This is packed in a very thin container which, as the consigner is aware, may well not contain the gas for the full distance for which it is consigned, and certainly will not do so if the train should strike any real trouble, for example, if the train should be derailed or involved in a collision, or if some passenger should interfere inadvertently or deliberately with the freight, perhaps trying to steal some of it. All of these sorts of things have happened on some previous journeys. If the container should break, the resulting disaster would probably kill at least some of the people on the train in adjacent carriages, while others could be maimed or poisoned or sooner or later incur serious diseases.

Most of us would roundly condemn such an action. What might the consigner of the parcel say to try to justify it?

Source: Richard and Val Routley (also known as Richard Sylvan and Val Plumwood). "Nuclear Power—Some Ethical and Social Dimensions." In *And Justice for All: New Introductory Essays in Ethics and Public Policy.* Tom Regan and Donald Van De Veer, eds. Totowa, NJ: Rowman & Allanheld, 1982. 116–138. 116–117.

The Routleys propose this thought experiment in order to test whether or not the development of nuclear power can be ethically justified. According to the authors, the facts about nuclear waste mean that "40,000 generations of future people could be forced to bear significant risks" (118)—loss of life, widespread disease and genetic damage, and contamination of immense areas of land. One possible justification, then, would be that we do not have any moral obligation to those future people (those who will be on the train as it travels onward). *Do* we? (Based on their rights? Can people who do not exist have rights? Based on promises made to them? Can we make promises to people who don't exist?) How much of an obligation? How far into the future? Must obligations to others be based on rights or promises, or is knowledge of the consequences of our actions sufficient to establish such obligations?

Even if we don't have an obligation to someone, does that mean we can do whatever we like to them? Perhaps the producer of the gas is not responsible for the train or the people on it, but isn't he or she responsible for the gas—and what it might *do to* the train and the people on it? One could say it's not certain the gas will escape or it's not certain what the consequences will be if it does. Do we need to be *certain* something will occur before we can say that risking its occurrence is morally unacceptable?

The apparent injustice of nuclear development might be justified, the authors suggest, if there are overriding circumstances. *Are* there? Perhaps the world needs the product in order to improve the standard of living, so it's the producer's duty to supply it; perhaps if the company afforded a better container, it would go bankrupt—jobs would be lost, families would be unsupported, and the whole company town would be worse off. The authors argue, however, that nuclear power is politically and economically inappropriate for raising the standard of living in the Third World; furthermore, the nuclear industry *increases,* rather than *decreases,* unemployment and poverty. Are there any other overriding circumstances that the consigner of the parcel might justifiably appeal to?

Regan's Lifeboat

Imagine five survivors are on a lifeboat. Because of limits of size, the boat can only support four. All weigh approximately the same and would take up approximately the same amount of space. Four of the five are normal adult human beings. The fifth is a dog. One must be thrown overboard or else all will perish. Who should it be?

Source: Tom Regan. *The Case for Animal Rights.* Berkeley: University of California Press, 1983. 285.

Regan argues that all individuals who are "subjects of a life" (who have interests and desires) have inherent value. And all individuals who have inherent value have, equally, the moral right to respectful and just treatment, which includes the right not to be harmed. Given that, should the occupants of the lifeboat draw straws to decide who goes overboard?

Regan says no—the dog goes. However, this is not because the dog is not a subject-of-a-life; it is such a subject and therefore has a right, equal to that of the human beings, to respectful and just treatment. Rather, argues Regan, it is because the death of one of the human beings would be a greater loss than the death of the dog, because more opportunities for the satisfaction of interests and desires would thus be lost. (So then they *don't* have an *equal* right to respectful and just treatment?)

Suppose then that there were five human beings (and no dog), one of whom had rather limited abilities and therefore few opportunities for the satisfaction of interests and desires. Should the same reasoning apply? (See "Godwin's Fenelon.")

Would the same reasoning permit scientific experimentation on a dog, or on a human being with limited ability, that would enable the development of a drug that would prevent the deaths of human beings with less limited abilities?

CASTE'S HEDONINE
AND PONONINE

Imagine that a legal drug was developed which I'll call "hedonine" and which worked by producing a clear-headed euphoria in the employee that allows him or her to enjoy their work while producing more efficiently. Now assume also that there were no long-term health risks associated with hedonine. It would seem to follow from the productivity argument that an employer would be justified in permitting or even *requiring* employees to take such a drug on a regular basis. . . .

. . .

. . . [Imagine further] a drug . . . (call it "pononine") which increases productivity but also produces painful side-effects. Since such a drug would affect an employee's productivity, its use would [also] be permissible by the productivity argument.

Source: Nicholas J. Caste. "Drug Testing and Productivity." *Journal of Business Ethics* 11.4 (1992): 301–306. 303.

Caste's intent with this thought experiment is to test the view that mandatory drug testing of employees is justified because of the negative effect drug use has on employee productivity. As Caste explains, "The productivity argument essentially states that since the employer has purchased the employee's time, the employer has a proprietary right to ensure that the time purchased is used as efficiently and productively as possible" (301).

If we want to say employers may *not* require employees to take hedonine or pononine, what amendment(s) must be made to the productivity argument? Or is there nothing objectionable about employers requiring their employees to take such drugs? (Does it matter if your employees are professional athletes?)

BATTIN'S AUTOMATIC REVERSIBLE CONTRACEPTION

What if everybody—all fertile females, and when the technology becomes available, all fertile males—were to use "automatic" reversible contraception?. . .

. . .

. . . One can imagine that . . . the use of these technologies might become a medical norm, the standard course of gynecological treatment for all adolescent and adult women, and eventually the medical norm for men as well—a health measure much like immunization, to which consent is perhaps superficially solicited but in practice assumed. One can even imagine such technologies—much like routine immunization—required for school entrance, at the junior high or high school level, for both girls and boys. "This is just what I do for all my patients," we can imagine the adolescent medicine or ob/gyn physician of the future saying, "I'm just helping them—especially the teenagers—protect themselves from pregnancy or siring pregnancy if they don't want it yet. I vaccinate them against typhoid and diphtheria and polio, and I immunize them against pregnancy—until they want it—too."

Source: Margaret P. Battin. "Sex & Consequences: World Population Growth vs. Reproductive Rights." *Philosophic Exchange* 27 (1997): 17-31. 17, 27-28.

Given that half of all pregnancies are unplanned, Battin assumes that "women—and parents generally—would *choose to have* fewer children than they would *accept having* if pregnancy occurred" (25). As things are, she explains, pregnancy is "the default mode"—unless one *does* something (for example, uses contraception), pregnancy will occur as a result of sexual intercourse during fertile periods about 20 percent of the time. But if one reversed the default mode—"if a woman [could] become pregnant only when she has made a choice to do so, a choice followed by removal or neutralization of her 'automatic' contraceptive device" (25)—many unwanted pregnancies would not occur in the first place, because women would be "far less vulnerable to being pressured, coerced, or overcome by passion in compromising sexual situations and hence risk pregnancy when that has not been her previously considered choice" (25–26). And men would be "protected from the effects of any impulsive or careless decisions or actions on her part that might affect his own reproductive freedom" (26)—protection which would have "substantial impact on paternity issues" (26). Battin's thought experiment demonstrates that there is a single solution to two contemporary problems: reversing the default mode "would not only result in potentially dramatic decreases in population growth, but . . . would substantially enhance both male and female reproductive freedom" (28).

Would Battin's suggestion provide the benefits she expects? And would the problems of increasing population and decreasing reproductive freedom be, therefore, solved?

Locke's Acorns and Apples

He that is nourished by the acorns he picked up under an oak, or the apples he gathered from the trees in the wood, has certainly appropriated them to himself. Nobody can deny but the nourishment is his. I ask, then, When did they begin to be his—when he digested, or when he ate, or when he boiled, or when he brought them home, or when he picked them up?

Source: John Locke. *An Essay Concerning the True Original, Extent and End of Civil Government* (the second of *Two Treatises of Government*). Chapter 5, Section 28. 1690. As reprinted in *The English Philosophers from Bacon to Mill*. Edwin A. Burtt, ed. New York: Random House, 1967. 403–503. 414.

Locke claims it is the gathering of the acorns and apples that makes them his, thus articulating the principle that one owns the results of one's labor: by doing something to what occurs in nature, you make it your private property; until then, it is common property. But if until then the acorns and apples were common property, should he have obtained the consent of others before he gathered them—"Was it a robbery thus to assume to himself what belonged to all in common?" (414). (See "Hardin's Tragedy of the Commons.")

And what of land ownership? If someone buys the land with the oak and apple trees on it, does that person therefore *own* the acorns and apples? He or she has "done" nothing—neither planted the trees nor, let's assume, taken care of them in any way. *Can* land be purchased and thus owned according to Locke's view? And if so, even so, do the acorns and apples belong to the people who actually take care of the trees (instead of whoever "owns" the land)?

And do these, should these, questions apply as much to air and water as to soil?

THE PRISONER'S DILEMMA

Imagine that you and another person are caught at the scene of a crime and subsequently interrogated separately by the police, who offer you the following deal. If neither of you confess to committing the crime, both of you will be charged with a lesser crime and serve a prison sentence of one year. If both of you confess, implicating each other, both of you will serve a sentence of ten years. However, if one of you confesses and the other one doesn't, the one who confesses will go free, while the one implicated by the confession will serve twenty years.

Will you confess?

Source: Attributed to Albert W. Tucker by S. J. Hagenmayer (*Philadelphia Inquirer,* February 2, 1995), who described a speech given by Tucker in 1950 (as per Roger A. McCain at http://william-king.www.drexel.edu/top/eco/game/dilemma.html). Original articulation not available.

Though created to illustrate the difficulty of analyzing games (note that no mention is made about whether you actually committed the crime), the Prisoner's Dilemma has been used by philosophers to examine sociopolitical questions. If the two people are rational and self-interested, they may each reason in this way: "If the other person confesses, I'll get either twenty years (if I don't confess) or ten years (if I do confess), and if the other person doesn't confess, I'll get either one year (if I don't confess) or no years (if I do confess)—in both cases, I'm better off if I confess." However, if they *both* reason along those lines, they'll *both* confess—in which case, they'll both be worse off (each getting ten years instead of, if they'd both not confessed, only one year). Thus, much like Hardin's tragedy of the commons (see "Hardin's Tragedy of the Commons"), acting according to one's own interests (approaching the decision as if you're the only one involved?), if and when done by everyone, turns out *not* to be in one's own interests.

But *would* rational self-interested people reason as described? What other lines of reasoning are possible? And what if, instead, we presupposed rational community-interested people?

And what if—as is the case for commons like our oceans, forests, and air (and as is the case in trade barrier and arms race decisions where similar reasoning may occur)—repeat actions are required: would that change the line of reasoning and hence the decisions?

Lastly, note the conditions of the thought experiment as given. First, there's no communication between the two people—what if they could and did talk to each other? Second, is the consequence arrangement fair, or at least realistic? How should we set up the game, or the world, if we want people who are admittedly most interested in their own well-being *not* to exploit each other? (See "Rawls's Veil of Ignorance" and "Nozick's Wilt Chamberlain.")

Hardin's Tragedy of the Commons

Picture a pasture open to all. . . .

As a rational being, each herdsman seeks to maximize his gain. Explicitly or implicitly, more or less consciously, he asks: "What is the utility *to me* of adding one more animal to my herd?". . . .

. . . Since the herdsman receives all the proceeds from the sale of the additional animal, the positive utility is nearly +1.

. . . Since, however, the effects of overgrazing are shared by all the herdsmen, the negative utility for any particular decision-making herdsman is only a fraction of −1.

. . . [T]he rational herdsman concludes that the only sensible course for him to pursue is to add another animal to his herd. And another; and another. . . . But this is the conclusion reached by each and every rational herdsman sharing a commons. Therein is the tragedy. Each man is locked in to a system that compels him to increase his herd without limit—in a world that is limited. Ruin is the destination toward which all men rush, each pursuing his own best interest in a society that believes in the freedom of the commons. Freedom in a commons brings ruin to all.

Source: Garrett Hardin. "The Tragedy of the Commons." *Science* 162 (1968): 1243–1248. 1244.

In 1776 Adam Smith claimed that those who pursue only their own interests are "led by an invisible hand to promote . . . the public interest" (*The Wealth of Nations*). Hardin's tragedy of the commons[1] serves as a rebuttal to Smith's "invisible hand": Hardin's herdsmen, pursuing only their own interests, do *not* in so doing promote the public interest. Consider not only the resulting overgrazed pastures, which can eventually feed no cows at all, but also the overfished oceans, which operate on the commons system; consider also pollution, which is, Hardin suggests, a sort of reverse tragedy of the commons.

But is it, as Hardin says, the freedom in a commons that brings ruin to all? Or is it, instead, the desire to maximize one's own gain or the tendency not to see beyond the short term? Furthermore, is the scenario Hardin describes best characterized by freedom—or injustice? *My* cow becomes fat eating *our* grass—so why should *I* get to keep all the money when I sell it? There seems to be a freedom here without a corresponding responsibility.

So is the solution to privatize the commons so that each person has his own little pasture? Or is the solution to socialize the system so that both pasture and cattle are held in common? Is there some third, or fourth, alternative? And will each system work equally well under all conditions (for example, population size and distribution, resource quantity and quality, and existing sociopolitical policies)?

Lastly, Hardin's thought experiment seems to suggest that sometimes an individual's action is morally wrong *only when* other people do the same thing; that is, it's not what *you* do that puts you "in the wrong"—it's what *other* people do. How can that be so (when what you do, your individual action, is the same whether you alone do it or whether others do it, too)?

---

[1] It is based on a scenario described by William Forster Lloyd in 1833 (*Two Lectures on the Checks to Population*, reprinted in Hardin's *Population Evolution and Birth Control*).

Rawls's Veil of Ignorance

Thus we are to imagine that those who engage in social cooperation choose together, in one joint act, the principles which are to assign basic rights and duties and to determine the division of social benefits. . . .

. . . This original position . . . is understood as a purely hypothetical situation characterized so as to lead to a certain conception of justice. Among the essential features of this situation is that no one knows his place in society, his class position or social status, nor does any one know his fortune in the distribution of natural assets and abilities, his intelligence, strength, and the like. I shall even assume that the parties do not know their conceptions of the good or their special psychological propensities. The principles of justice are chosen behind a veil of ignorance. This ensures that no one is advantaged or disadvantaged in the choice of principles by the outcome of natural chance or the contingency of social circumstances. Since all are similarly situated and no one is able to deign principles to favor his particular condition, the principles of justice are the result of a fair agreement or bargain.

What principles of justice would be chosen?

Source: John Rawls. *A Theory of Justice.* Cambridge, MA: Harvard University Press, 1971. 11, 12.

Rawls claims that "free and rational persons concerned to further their own interests" (11) would, from behind the veil of ignorance he describes, agree to the following principle as a "blueprint" for their society: "All social values—liberty and opportunity, income and wealth, and the bases of self-respect—are to be distributed equally unless an unequal distribution of any, or all, of these values is to everyone's advantage" (62). One might concede that people will choose basic equality in case it turns out they're the ones not so fortunate with regard to natural assets and abilities; one might also concede that people will permit inequality in case they *are* fortunate—so they can take advantage of their superior resources. But what principle could have been agreed to instead? One possibility is the Marxian "to each according to his or her need"; another is "to each as he or she is entitled" (see "Nozick's Wilt Chamberlain"); yet another is the utilitarian "greatest good for the greatest number." Which of these will result in a just society? (See "Marty's Two Shipwrecked Islanders.")

Critics of Rawls have pointed out the difficulty, and even the impossibility, of making decisions about rights, duties, and social benefits when one's values ("conceptions of the good") are unknown. Furthermore, insofar as where you end up depends on where you start, one might ask why Rawls postulates only self-interested people—what sort of society would communally interested people come up with?

NOZICK'S WILT CHAMBERLAIN

Now suppose that Wilt Chamberlain is greatly in demand by basketball teams, being a great gate attraction. (Also suppose contracts run only for a year, with players being free agents.) He signs the following sort of contract with a team: in each home game, twenty-five cents from the price of each ticket of admission goes to him. (We ignore the question of whether he is "gouging" the owners, letting them look out for themselves.) The season starts, and people cheerfully attend his team's games; they buy their tickets, each time dropping a separate twenty-five cents of their admission price into a special box with Chamberlain's name on it. They are excited about seeing him play; it is worth the total admission price to them. Let us suppose that in one season one million persons attend his home games, and Wilt Chamberlain winds up with $250,000, a much larger sum than the average income and larger even than anyone else has. Is he entitled to this income?

Source: Robert Nozick. *Anarchy, State, and Utopia.* New York: Basic Books, 1974. 161.

Nozick's "Wilt Chamberlain" is part of a much larger discussion about the nature of the state—about what sort of government is best and how limitations on individual rights can be justified. Those who advocate a rather extensive government claim that such a government is necessary in order to achieve "distributive justice" (the fair distribution of goods within a society). Many theories of just distribution look at the "end result" (that is, who ends up with what) and determine justice in accord with, say, need or merit. But in such an "end result" system, Nozick says, people would have to be prevented from or compensated for freely chosen transfers of goods (since such transfers probably wouldn't always result in the desired end), and this would imply continuous "state intervention" and limitations on individual rights.

Nozick claims that fair distribution (or "holding," as Nozick prefers to say since goods are not in some ownerless pile waiting to be distributed by someone) is possible with a less extensive government—"a minimal state" that requires less violation of rights. According to his "entitlement theory," both the original acquisitions of goods and their transfers between people are justified if they accord with "entitlement": "From each according to what he chooses to do, to each according to what he makes for himself (perhaps with the contracted aid of others) and what others choose to do for him and choose to give him of what they've been given previously (under this maxim) and haven't yet expended or transferred" (160). (See "Locke's Acorns and Apples.")

His Wilt Chamberlain scenario is a description of such a system at work. If you say, "Yes, Chamberlain *is* entitled to the income"—since people voluntarily *choose* to give him their twenty-five cents (twenty-five cents they had justly in their possession) and since the income of the other players is not thereby diminished—then you are agreeing with Nozick and other libertarians in their claim that distributive justice *can* be achieved *without* government intervention and the consequent violation of individual rights.

But perhaps you might say Chamberlain is *not* entitled to that $250,000. Why not? Rawls would say the unequal distribution of income is unfair because it is not to everyone's advantage. (See "Rawls's Veil of Ignorance.") Are there other answers?

One might point out that Nozick's view assumes that people are equally free or equally able to make voluntary choices. Is that realistic? One might also ask how people come to have the resources—mental and physical ability, effort, skill, raw materials—to make whatever it is Nozick says they're thus entitled to.

Hardin's Lifeboat

Here we sit, say 50 people in a lifeboat. To be generous, let us assume our boat has a capacity of 10 more, making 60. . . .

The 50 of us in the lifeboat see 100 others swimming in the water outside, asking for admission to the boat, or for handouts. How shall we respond to their calls?

Source: Garrett Hardin. "Living on a Lifeboat." *BioScience* 24 (October 1974): 561–568. 562.

This scenario is presented by Hardin as a metaphor for the framework within which we must work out solutions to the problems of overpopulation and hunger: each lifeboat is a rich nation full of comparatively rich people, and in the ocean swim the poor of the world, having fallen out of their more crowded lifeboats. (See "O'Neill's Lifeboat.")

Hardin first considers this option: "We may be tempted to try to live by the Christian ideal of being 'our brother's keeper,' or by the Marxian ideal of 'from each according to his abilities, to each according to his needs.' Since the needs of all are the same, we take all the needy into our boat, making a total of 150 in a boat with a capacity of 60. The boat is swamped, and everyone drowns. Complete justice, complete catastrophe" (562). Furthermore, as Hardin points out, "needs . . . are determined by population size, which is affected by reproduction [and] every nation regards its rate of reproduction as a sovereign right" (562). So perhaps a better solution is to stop considering the right to reproduce *as* a right, or at least as an *unassailable* right.

Next, Hardin suggests that "since the boat has an unused excess capacity of 10, we admit just 10 more to it. This has the disadvantage of getting rid of the safety factor [a new plant disease or a bad change in the weather may decimate our population if we don't preserve some excess capacity as a safety factor], for which action we will sooner or later pay dearly. Moreover, *which* 10 do we let in? 'First come, first served?' The best 10? The neediest 10? How do we *discriminate?* And what do we say to the 90 who are excluded?" (562). Accordingly, perhaps we should consider whether the poor swimming in the ocean *deserve* to be poor. (And whether *we* deserve to be rich and in the boat?)

Lastly, Hardin suggests that we "admit no more to the boat and preserve the small safety factor. Survival of the people in the lifeboat is then possible (though we shall have to be on our guard against boarding parties)" (562). Is that fair? Is it right? Is it (nevertheless) what we should do? (And are the results of Hardin's thought experiment applicable to real life—*are* we living in a lifeboat? . . .)

O'NEILL'S LIFEBOAT

Let us imagine six survivors on a lifeboat. There are two possible levels of provisions:

1. [On the well-equipped lifeboat,] provisions are on all reasonable calculations sufficient to last until rescue. Either the boat is near land, or it is amply provisioned, or it has gear for distilling water, catching fish, etc.

2. [On the underequipped lifeboat,] provisions are on all reasonable calculations unlikely to be sufficient for all six to survive until rescue.

When would killing be justified?

Source: Onora O'Neill. "Lifeboat Earth." *Philosophy & Public Affairs* 4.3 (Spring 1975): 273–292. 276–277.

If we imagine," O'Neill continues, "a lifeboat in which special quarters are provided for the (recently) first-class passengers, and on which the food and water for all passengers are stowed in those quarters, then we have a fair, if crude, model of the present human situation on lifeboat Earth" (280–281). (See "Hardin's Lifeboat.") Since people are dying on Earth because of our distribution of food and water, either we concede that their deaths are unjustifiable (for they have not occurred as a result of self-defense and they have been avoidable) or we claim that property rights (presumably such people have been deemed to have no right to said food and water) do indeed trump the right not to be killed. Which is it?

Perhaps, however, our situation is more like the underequipped lifeboat. But if *we* are responsible for the lifeboat *being* underequipped, O'Neill argues, again, we cannot say the deaths from lack of food and water are unavoidable. Who *is* responsible for the lifeboat's condition? (And who is going to rescue us?)

ALEXANDER'S DOOMSDAY MACHINE

Assume there is a super-sophisticated satellite that can detect all criminal acts and determine the mental state of the actors. (The society that has invented this device has made criminal only those acts that are clearly violations of the moral rights of others.) If the satellite finds that the actor knew his act was a crime, that he had no recognized excuse or justification for committing it, that he was not acting in the heat of passion or under duress, and that he was not too young, enfeebled, mentally unbalanced, and so forth to be deemed without capacity to commit a crime, the satellite immediately—and without regard to the seriousness of the crime—zaps him with a disintegration ray. Once the satellite detects the crime, it is impossible to prevent punishment of the criminal, no matter how merciful the authorities might feel. The definitions of crimes and the punishments attached thereto can be changed only prospectively. The entire population is informed of the existence of the satellite and what it does.

Now . . . is the punishment meted out by my imaginary device (the Doomsday Machine . . .)—obliteration for all crimes committed with certain mental states, right down to intentional overparking—excessive?

Source: Lawrence Alexander. "The Doomsday Machine: Proportionality, Punishment and Prevention." *The Monist* 63.2 (1980): 199–227. 209. Copyright © 1980, The Hegeler Institute.

A lexander anticipates that we will think the punishment meted out by the Doomsday Machine is excessive. Believing our response to be mistaken, he presents the following hypothetical scenario (209–210):

> Suppose a man receives a phone call from a burglar who says, "I've been spying on you and know you're going out tonight. I plan to burglarize your house in order to steal your valuables. But I want you to know that I have a very bad heart, and if you hide your valuables, I might very well suffer a heart attack by expending a lot of energy and suffering anxiety in looking for them. So please leave them in plain sight; for I am definitely going to enter you house and look for them until I find them or drop dead." The listener hangs up the phone, takes his valuables, hides them on the very top shelf of his closet, and leaves. He returns home and finds the burglar, dead from a heart attack, on the floor.

Alexander believes we will *not* consider *this* to be a case of excessive punishment despite having the following in common with the Doomsday Machine: a person intends to do wrong, the person is aware that by doing so he risks losing his life, and no human intervention to prevent his death is possible. So, to be consistent, if we don't consider the burglary to be a case of excessive punishment, we can't consider the Doomsday Machine to be a case of excessive punishment.

Alexander argues that both the Doomsday Machine and the burglary case are "instances of the *enterprise of prevention,* an enterprise that . . . appears to be morally justifiable when conducted according to certain principles, among which is *not* the principle of proportionality" (213). The principle of proportionality, he argues, is relevant only when punishment is intended as an *enterprise of retribution*—a matter of meting out what is *deserved.*

It follows, Alexander says (214–215), that

> the sheriff of a small town where the courthouse lawn is trespassed upon by five hundred sitting sunbathers need not restrict himself to force proportionate to the wrong of trespassing in order to remove the trespassers. . . . He may, instead, place a machine gun on the roof of the courthouse, inform the sunbathers that the machine gun is programmed to begin spraying the lawn in five minutes, and leave. . . . Moreover, if the sheriff can set up the *automatic* machine gun, then conceivably it would follow that he could man the machine gun; and if he could man the machine gun, then it would seem to follow that the town council could pass a new trespass ordinance mandating death by machine gunning as the punishment.

Has something gone wrong here?

Marty's Two Shipwrecked Islanders

[T]wo men are ship-wrecked on an island. One works hard. He plows the ground, plants seed, weeds his field, chases the birds away, waters the crop through the heat and dryness of summer, builds a shed to store the grain through the blizzards of winter, builds himself a cabin to survive the cold, and then harvests the crop. The other man, by happenstance formerly a hit man, acts differently. Through the hot summer he sits in the shade of the tree, swims in the pleasant lagoon, and lives idly off the fat of the land for the living is easy, and besides, when winter comes, he plans to knock the other man on the head while he sleeps and take his grain, his shed, and his shelter. This man neither makes a crop, thereby earning his keep, nor has he the good in his heart.

Now to whom, in this hypothetical situation, does that store of grain rightly belong?

Source: William R. Marty. "Rawls and the Harried Mother." *Interpretation* 9.2–3 (1982): 385–396. 387–388. Copyright © 1982 Interpretation. Reprinted by permission.

Marty hopes this thought experiment will show that Rawls's concept of distributive justice is not a good one (see Rawls's "Veil of Ignorance"). According to Rawls, Marty says, the grain should be divided equally; that is what the two men would determine to be a fair arrangement if their decision is made, as Rawls would have it, from behind a veil of ignorance—not knowing by whom the grain came to be produced. But, Marty claims, surely our intuition says that such an arrangement would be *un*fair; surely the grain belongs to the one who worked hard to produce it (see "Locke's Acorns and Apples").

Marty argues with a second thought experiment that Rawls's method leads only to a *self-interested* arrangement, not to a *just* arrangement (388):

> Suppose now our two islanders are told that one produced the grain and one did not. How then would they divide the grain [according to Rawls]? Still equally, because neither would know who had produced the grain and who had not, and in any case, neither could afford to distribute it on the basis of desert because that would give a fifty percent chance of getting the zero share, which would mean he would not survive the winter. . . . [E]ach islander would know that one deserved the grain and one did not. They would know that an equal distribution is not a just distribution. But that would have no influence on their decision because they are making a rational calculation of their self-interest in dividing the grain, not a rational assessment of what a just distribution of the grain would be. Since the two are not the same, the result of the Rawlsian scheme is not, except by coincidence or definition, justice.

"Rawls's distribution is faulty," says Marty, "because it divorces distribution from a number of things that can legitimately give a claim to a particular share of a distribution" (388). Among these things are contribution, effort, risk, need, skill, and responsibility.

But suppose the idle islander does do a bit of planting and weeding but has a tapeworm and is therefore too weak to work as hard as the other and, furthermore, because of the tapeworm, requires more grain than the other for sustenance. How should the grain then be divided? That is, when the elements suggested by Marty conflict (in this case, contribution conflicts with need, and the element of ability is added to complicate contribution), which element counts more?

Parfit's Nobelist

Suppose that a man aged ninety, one of the few rightful holders of the Nobel Peace Prize, confesses that it was he who, at the age of twenty, injured a policeman in a drunken brawl.

Does this man now deserve to be punished?

Source: Derek Parfit. *Reasons and Persons.* Oxford, UK: Oxford University Press, 1986. 326.

If identity depends on physical continuity (see "Williams's Charles and Guy Fawkes—and Robert"), then the man does not deserve to be punished, because by the age of ninety, not one cell in his brain or body is the same as it was at the age of twenty. But would that be true if he had committed the crime at fifty or seventy? (As the time between the commission of a crime and the punishment increases, should the severity of the punishment decrease?) And which cells exactly are we interested in?

If identity depends on psychological continuity independent of the brain and body (see "Shoemaker's Brownson"), then perhaps the man does deserve to be punished. Certainly, since he remembered committing the crime, he has continuity in that respect (see "Locke's Prince and Cobbler"). So if we can't remember (or have forgotten) doing something, we can't be held responsible for it?

What about psychological continuity not of memory but of beliefs, desires, and so on? It is quite likely that at ninety, we will not have the same beliefs and desires we had at twenty. Indeed, this man has become a *Peace* Prize winner—surely he doesn't believe in assaulting police officers anymore. So he does not deserve to be punished? (But if you are not tomorrow who you are today, why should you care about what happens to you tomorrow? See "Williams's Body Exchange/Mind Swap.")

What about psychological continuity with regard to character or personality—is that different from or independent of one's beliefs and desires? Could the man have the same personality without having the same beliefs and desires? And would he then deserve to be punished?

It is the presence of free will that often justifies desert (that is, whether something is deserved), and hence punishment. Wherein lies free will—is it part of one's body or brain and/or part of one's character or personality?

Perhaps it is helpful to consider reasons for punishment other than desert. For example, if the purpose of punishment is deterrence, then perhaps the man, whether he is the same man or not, does not deserve to be punished.

MILLS'S MR. OREO

Consider the case of someone I will call Mr. Oreo. Mr. Oreo cannot even think of passing, being quite dark with clearly black African features and with known black ancestry. But he is unhappy with his racial designation, so he fills in "white" on bureaucratic forms, identifies himself as white, and rejects black culture. Will these gestures make him white? . . .

Suppose individuals such as Mr. Oreo whose bodies are *not* . . . naturally white make use of [plastic surgery techniques or genetic engineering that make it possible to transform one's skin, hair, and facial features so that one looks completely white] and then go on to assimilate as above. [Would they *be* white or just look white?] . . . Compare another kind of physical transformation, that of bodily physique and strength. If a machine were invented (call this the Schwartzeneggar Machine) that could transform 98-pound weaklings into massively muscled supermen capable of pressing hundreds of pounds without the tedium of years of special diets and weight training, would we say that the person only *looked* strong but had not really *become* strong? Obviously not: his new body, new physique, new strength are real. So what is the difference?

Source: Charles W. Mills. *Blackness Visible: Essays on Philosophy and Race.* Ithaca, NY: Cornell University Press, 1998. 60, 61. Copyright © 1998 by Cornell University.

One of the intuitions Mills tries to undermine with this thought experiment is that one's race is permanent. He lists various criteria used to designate race—physical appearance, ancestry, awareness of ancestry by self, awareness of ancestry by others, culture, experience, and self-identity—and shows through a series of cases how we seem to be quite "flexible" about how we determine what one "really" is. Mr. Oreo would be considered black because of his physical appearance, but when he changes his physical appearance so that he appears white, he'll still be considered "really" to be black, now because of his ancestry. And yet the similarly transformed weakling is not still considered to be "really" a weakling. *Is* there a difference or are we just inconsistent in our racial designations? If race is, as Mills argues, whatever we as a society think it is, then perhaps the Mr. Oreo who undergoes plastic surgery and genetic engineering and lives in "white culture" *is* now white. . . .

DEWEY'S FINELY WROUGHT OBJECT

Suppose . . . that a finely wrought object, one whose texture and proportions are highly pleasing in perception, has been believed to be a product of some primitive people. Then there is discovered evidence that proves it to be an accidental natural product. . . .

Is it a work of art?

Source: John Dewey. *Art as Experience*. New York: Capricorn Books, 1934. 48.

Dewey claims that even though the object is precisely what it was before the discovery, immediately upon such discovery, "it ceases to be a work of art" (48) and "belongs in a museum of natural history, not in a museum of art" (48). Why? His answer is that to qualify as art, a work must be "framed for enjoyed receptive perception" (48). Mere technique or virtuosity on the part of the artist is not enough, but neither is simply being perceived. What is important, says Dewey, is the *relation* between "doing and undergoing" (48), the *connection* between production and reception: "The doing or making is artistic when the perceived result is of such a nature that *its* qualities *as perceived* have controlled the question of production" (48). Furthermore, just as the artist must create with the perception always in mind, the beholder must perceive with the creation in mind.

So what if that connection were intended but failed to occur—what if, for example, a listener didn't hear what it was the musician intended to be heard? Is that just bad art? Failed art? Nonart?

And what if no connection were intended—what if someone painted a painting, then wrapped it up immediately and sent it into outer space never to be seen by anyone?

ZIFF'S ECCENTRIC AND PECULIAR OBJECTS

Suppose an object were found, satisfying the conditions given above [deliberate production, production for display and contemplation, actual exhibition in a museum gallery, the presence of certain formal features such as unity and variety, the presence of a definite subject matter, and so on], but with this one eccentricity: the scene depicted, and consequently the formal structure as well, changed periodically, without being changed. Imagine [another] object fitting the description, but having the peculiarity that, without being moved, it moved occasionally about the room. Thus in a way these odd objects behave somewhat like living organisms.

Are these objects works of art?

Source: Paul Ziff. "The Task of Defining a Work of Art." *Philosophical Review* 62.1 (1953): 58–78. 63.

Ziff uses this thought experiment to illustrate the difficulty of defining "work of art." We would be reluctant to call the eccentric and peculiar objects he describes works of art, he says, even though they satisfy all the conditions listed. Thus Ziff shows that attempts to define art with a set of conditions are unsuccessful.

So too, he argues, are attempts to define works of art by establishing their similarity to some characteristic work of art. The problem with this approach is that "no rule can be given to determine what is or is not a sufficient degree of similarity" (65). For example, a Greek vase may be similar enough to a Poussin painting to be considered a work of art: they are both exhibited, they both have formal features, and they both have a definite subject matter. None of this is true for a New England bean pot. And yet, the bean pot is similar to the vase: both were made for domestic purposes, and neither was intended for display. Furthermore, at the time of its creation, the vase was not exhibited. So why are the painting and the vase considered art, but the bean pot not?

Ziff goes on to consider whether this difficulty with definition matters—why do we want or need a clear definition of "work of art"? Certainly, it is important to be understood when one uses a certain phrase, and clear definitions enable that understanding. But perhaps more to the point is to ask "What are the consequences and implications of something's being considered a work of art?" (72). And are those consequences and implications dependent on context of place and time?

Danto's Randomly Generated Object

Imagine that we learned that the object before us [which] looks like a painting that would spontaneously move us if we believed it had been painted—say the *Polish Rider* of Rembrandt, in which an isolated mounted figure is shown midjourney to an uncertain destiny—was not painted at all but is the result of someone's having dumped lots of paint in a centrifuge, giving the contrivance a spin, and having the result splat onto canvas, "just to see what would happen." . . . Now the question is whether, knowing this fact, we are prepared to consider this randomly generated object a work of art.

Source: Arthur C. Danto. *The Transfiguration of the Commonplace.* Cambridge, MA: Harvard University Press, 1981. 31.

Is the randomly generated object a work of art if someone declares it to be? Then is the Rembrandt painting a work of art for the same reason?

Or is the Rembrandt painting a work of art because it was created by an artist and the other object wasn't? Is this why a painting of a person's face is a work of art but the person's face is not? But not everything created by an artist is art. . . . And what exactly makes someone an artist?

Or is the randomly generated object *not* a work of art, because it lacks certain elements? Such as a certain intent on the part of the creator or a certain response on the part of the viewer? (See "Dewey's Finely Wrought Object.") What if a painting is accidentally destroyed before anyone can see it? Or what if the response were unremarkable, if everyone mistook the randomly generated piece for part of the wall on which it hung? (What if that was the case for the Rembrandt?)

If we are prepared to say that the randomly generated object *is* a work of art because of its *intrinsic* qualities (for example, design, color, and so on), then must we also say it doesn't matter if a work of art is the "original" or an indistinguishable "fake" or "duplicate" (that is, an exact copy with regard to design, color, and so on)? Indeed, if works of art can be so perfectly duplicated, perhaps it doesn't even make sense to talk about "originals." (Would that apply not only to questions of aesthetic identity but also to questions of personal identity? See "Parfit's Teletransporter." Or should artifacts be considered differently from organisms? See "Price's *E. coli* John.")

MOORE'S GLASS FLOWERS

The collection [of glass flowers at Harvard University] comprises more than eight hundred exquisitely fashioned models, ranging from truly exotic plants, scarcely ever seen, to common weeds. Invariably, viewers are powerfully impressed by the lifelike quality of the models. In fact, . . . it would be nearly impossible to tell which was glass and which was a real flower if a model and its subject were placed side by side.

One of the specimens represented is *Chicorium intybus*, common chicory. This is a delicate roadside wildflower, common throughout North America. Its long, straight, striated stalks are festooned with star clusters of short, triangular leaves and compact, blue, daisylike flowers. . . . Now suppose that, having been struck by the beauty of the glass chicory specimen, a museum visitor were to walk outside and discover at the parking lot's edge a living chicory plant, a plant whose physical differences from that of the glass plant were visually indiscernible. Having found the man-made chicory beautiful, should the viewer, to be consistent, . . . find the live chicory equally beautiful?

Source: Ronald Moore. "Appreciating Natural Beauty as Natural." *Journal of Aesthetic Education* 33.3 (1999): 42–59. 45.

M oore suspects that most of us would regard the roadside chicory as less beautiful than the glass one. But, he says, "won't that be because we are implicitly counting the factors of illusion, hard work, and rarity into our assessment of the glass flower's beauty? [And] aren't these factors contributors to the model's worth in ways other than in respect of beauty?" (45).

Moore then approaches the matter from the other direction: he imagines an artificial chicory indistinguishable from the real thing (it even has the same scent and taste) and suspects that our response to the artificial one, once we are informed it *is* artificial, will be one of disappointment and perhaps even disdain. "But," he asks, "what is it, exactly, about the thought that a thing emanated from natural process rather than human manufacture (which is, after all, just one more attenuated form of natural process, if you take the human participation in the great chain of being seriously) that should render our contemplation of it so immediately pleasing and valuable?" (47).

Moore's thought experiment demonstrates that we seem to use different standards of beauty for natural objects than we do for nonnatural objects (with the paradoxical result that sometimes the natural object is perceived to be more beautiful and sometimes less beautiful than the nonnatural object). What could justify these different standards?

CARROLL'S LOATHE LETTER

Imagine that you have just broken up with your lover. You despise your ex-lover now. You sit down and write a letter to express your disdain. It's a long letter, written in publicly accessible language, and you use the space to clarify your emotions colorfully. It's individualized in the sense that you dwell graphically on the specific wrongs dealt to you. It's a very effective letter. You make your lover loathe himself/herself in the same way that you loathe him or her. And that's what you intended. But I doubt we would regard most such letters as art; nor if you told your lover off in this way while standing by the company microwave, I doubt we would view it as part of the history of drama.

Source: Noël Carroll. *Philosophy of Art: A Contemporary Introduction.* London: Routledge, 1999. 78.

With this thought experiment, Carroll tests the adequacy of the expression theory of art. The loathe letter meets the required conditions: it is an intentional expression of examined and clarified emotion (individualized and experienced emotion) to an audience by means of lines, colors, sounds, shapes, actions, and/or words. Nevertheless, we wouldn't call it art. (Nor would we call the microwave moment "art" even though it too meets the conditions.) This proves, Carroll claims, that the expressive theory is inadequate. (Unless, of course, we decide the letter is art after all.) So should the theory be rejected or modified? If the latter, what condition could be added that would eliminate the letter from the sphere of art?

PATTON'S CAN BAD MEN MAKE GOOD BRAINS DO BAD THINGS?

On Twin Earth, a brain in a vat is at the wheel of a runaway trolley. There are only two options that the brain can take: the right side of the fork in the track or the left side of the fork. There is no way in sight of derailing or stopping the trolley and the brain is aware of this, for the brain *knows* trolleys. The brain is causally hooked up to the trolley such that the brain can determine the course which the trolley will take.

On the right side of the track there is a single railroad worker, Jones, who will definitely be killed if the brain steers the trolley to the right. If the railman on the right lives, he will go on to kill five men for the sake of killing them, but in doing so will inadvertently save the lives of thirty orphans (one of the five men he will kill is planning to destroy a bridge that the orphan's bus will be crossing later that night). One of the orphans that will be killed would have grown up to become a tyrant who would make good utilitarian men do bad things. Another of the orphans would grow up to become G.E.M. Anscombe, while a third would invent the pop-top can.

If the brain in the vat chooses the left side of the track, the trolley will definitely hit and kill a railman on the left side of the track, "Leftie," and will hit and destroy ten beating hearts on the track that could (and would) have been transplanted into ten patients in the local hospital that will die without donor hearts. These are the only hearts available, and the

Source: Michael F. Patton, Jr. "Can Bad Men Make Good Brains Do Bad Things?" First published as "Tissues in the Profession: Can Bad Men Make Good Brains Do Bad Things?" In *Proceedings and Addresses of the American Philosophical Association* 61.3 (January 1988). Copyright © 1988 by the American Philosophical Association. Reprinted by permission. See also http://www.mindspring.com/~mfpatton/Tissues.htm.

brain is aware of this, for the brain *knows* hearts. If the railman on the left side of the track lives, he too will kill five men, in fact the same five that the railman on the right would kill. However, "Leftie" will kill the five as an unintended consequence of saving ten men: he will inadvertently kill the five men rushing the ten hearts to the local hospital for transplantation. A further result of "Leftie's" act would be that the busload of orphans will be spared. Among the five men killed by "Leftie" are both the man responsible for putting the brain at the controls of the trolley, and the author of this example. If the ten hearts and "Leftie" are killed by the trolley, the ten prospective heart-transplant patients will die and their kidneys will be used to save the lives of twenty kidney-transplant patients, one of whom will grow up to cure cancer, and one of whom will grow up to be Hitler. There are other kidneys and dialysis machines available; however, the brain does not *know* kidneys, and this is not a factor.

Assume that the brain's choice, whatever it turns out to be, will serve as an example to other brains-in-vats and so the effects of his decision will be amplified. Also assume that if the brain chooses the right side of the fork, an unjust war free of war crimes will ensue, while if the brain chooses the left fork, a just war fraught with war crimes will result. Furthermore, there is an intermittently active Cartesian demon deceiving the brain in such a manner that the brain is never sure if it is being deceived.

What should the brain do?

Index by Author

INDEX BY DATE
OF PUBLICATION

236

Index by Keyword

Predictor, 20; Taylor's Ingenious
Physiologist, 26

deterrence - Alexander's Doomsday
Machine, 214; Parfit's Nobelist, 218

double effect, doctrine of - Foot's Gas,
154

drug testing - Caste's Hedonine and
Pononine, 196

dualism - Kirk and Squires's Zombies,
52; Locke's Inverted Spectrum, 46. *See
also* Mind/body.

egoism - Feinberg's Egoist, 162. *See also*
Self-interest.

empiricism - Descartes's Evil Demon,
102; Hume's Constant Conjunction,
114; Hume's Missing Shade of Blue,
112; Kant's *A Priori* Space, 116;
Molyneux's Blind Man, 110. *See also*
Sensory experience.

environmental ethics - Hardin's
Lifeboat, 210; Hardin's Tragedy of the
Commons, 204; Locke's Acorns and
Apples, 200; The Routleys' Nuclear
Train, 192; Sylvan's Last People, 186

ethical decision making - Foot's Gas,
154; Jamieson and Regan's Chainsaw,
164; Jamieson and Regan's Terrorist
Tank, 166; Nozick's Experience
Machine, 160

euthanasia - Rachels's Smith and Jones
at the Bathtub, 188

evil, the problem of - Hick's World
with Flexible Laws of Nature, 40;
Hume's Infant, Inferior, or
Superannuated Deity, 32; Plantinga's
Curley Smith and Transworld Depravity,
42; Rowe's Fawn, 44

favoritism - Donaldson's Equim, 172;
Godwin's Fenelon, 148

form - Hobbes's Ship of Theseus, 68

free will - Frankfurt's Willing Addict,
24; Hick's World with Flexible Laws of
Nature, 40; James's Way Home, 18;
Locke's Voluntary Prisoner, 16; Lyon's

Card Predictor, 20; Parfit's Nobelist,
218; Plantinga's Curley Smith and
Transworld Depravity, 42; Taylor's
Ingenious Physiologist, 26

functional states, functionalism -
Block's Chinese Nation, 56; Locke's
Inverted Spectrum, 46; Searle's Brain
Replacement, 66

future people - The Routleys' Nuclear
Train, 192

gods, existence of - Berkeley's Impos-
sibility of Conceiving the Unconceived, 6;
Gaunilo's Lost Island, 28; Hick's
Resurrected People, 38; Hick's World with
Flexible Laws of Nature, 40; Nietzche's
Eternal Recurrence, 8; Paley's Watch, 34;
Pascal's Wager, 30; Rowe's Fawn, 44;
Wisdom's Long-Neglected Garden, 36

gods, nature of - Hume's Infant,
Inferior, or Superannuated Deity, 32;
Plantinga's Curley Smith and Transworld
Depravity, 42; Rowe's Fawn, 44

government - Nozick's Wilt
Chamberlain, 208

happiness - *see* Pleasure

harm to others - Foot's Gas, 154;
Harris's Survival Lottery, 190; Jamieson
and Regan's Chainsaw, 164; Jamieson
and Regan's Terrorist Tank, 166; Regan's
Lifeboat, 194; The Routleys' Nuclear
Train, 192; Sylvan's Last People, 186;
Thomson's Transplant Problem, 170;
Thomson's Trolley Problem, 168

hedonism - Moore's Two Worlds, 150;
Nozick's Experience Machine, 160

the ideal society - Hardin's Tragedy of
the Commons, 204; Nozick's Wilt
Chamberlain, 208; Plato's Ring of
Gyges, 146; The Prisoner's Dilemma,
202; Rawls's Veil of Ignorance, 206

identity - Black's Two Spheres, 142;
Hobbes's Ship of Theseus, 68; Price's *E.
coli* John, 84

identity, memory criterion - Leibniz's
King of China, 74; Locke's Prince and

Cobbler, 70; Perry's Divided Self, 82; Reid's Brave Officer, 72; Williams's Body Exchange/Mind Swap, 80; Williams's Charles and Guy Fawkes—and Robert, 76

identity, personal - Danto's Randomly Generated Object, 226; Hobbes's Ship of Theseus, 68; Leibniz's King of China, 74; Locke's Prince and Cobbler, 70; Parfit's Fission, 86; Parfit's Nobelist, 218; Parfit's Teletransporter, 88; Perry's Divided Self, 82; Price's *E. coli* John, 84; Reid's Brave Officer, 72; Shoemaker's Brownson, 78; Williams's Body Exchange/Mind Swap, 80; Williams's Charles and Guy Fawkes—and Robert, 76

identity, physical criterion - Hobbes's Ship of Theseus, 68; Locke's Prince and Cobbler, 70; Parfit's Nobelist, 218; Parfit's Teletransporter, 88; Price's *E. coli* John, 84; Shoemaker's Brownson, 78; Williams's Body Exchange/Mind Swap, 80; Williams's Charles and Guy Fawkes—and Robert, 76

identity, psychological criterion - Parfit's Nobelist, 218; Parfit's Teletransporter, 88; Shoemaker's Brownson, 78; Williams's Body Exchange/Mind Swap, 80

indeterminism - Taylor's Ingenious Physiologist, 26

infanticide - Tooley's Kitten, 180; Warren's Space Traveler, 182

infinity - Lucretius's Spear, 4; Zeno's Achilles, 2

innate ideas - Hume's Missing Shade of Blue, 112; Mill's Chaotic World, 118; Molyneux's Blind Man, 110; Plato's Equal Portions of Wood and Stone, 106

innocents, harming - Brandt's Spelunkers, 156; Harris's Survival Lottery, 190; Jamieson and Regan's Terrorist Tank, 166

intent - Foot's Gas, 154

inverted spectrum - Locke's Inverted Spectrum, 46

justice - Alexander's Doomsday Machine, 214; Brandt's Spelunkers, 156; Donaldson's Equim, 172; Godwin's Fenelon, 148; Hardin's Lifeboat, 210; Hardin's Tragedy of the Commons, 204; Marty's Two Shipwrecked Islanders, 216; Nozick's Wilt Chamberlain, 208; O'Neill's Lifeboat, 212; Parfit's Nobelist, 218; Plato's Ring of Gyges, 146; Regan's Lifeboat, 194; Rawls's Veil of Ignorance, 206

justification - Bonjour's Clairvoyants, 128; Goldman's Fake Barns, 126; Harman's False Report, 124; Plantinga's Epistemically Inflexible Climber, 130; Skyrms's Pyromaniac, 122

killing and letting die - O'Neill's Lifeboat, 212; Rachels's Smith and Jones at the Bathtub, 188; Thomson's Trolley Problem, 168; Williams's Jim in South America, 158

knowledge, conditions of - Bonjour's Clairvoyants, 128; Gettier's Smith and Jones (and Brown in Barcelona), 120; Goldman's Fake Barns, 126; Harman's False Report, 124; Lehrer's Mr. Truetemp, 132; Plantinga's Epistemically Inflexible Climber, 130; Skyrms's Pyromaniac, 122

knowledge, kinds of - Jackson's Mary, the Brilliant Color Scientist, 64

knowledge, limits of - Descartes's Evil Demon, 102; Kirk and Squires's Zombies, 52; Locke's Inverted Spectrum, 46; Nagel's Bat, 54

knowledge, possibility of - Descartes's Evil Demon, 102; Locke's Inverted Spectrum, 46; Nagel's Bat, 54; Putnam's Brain in a Vat, 62

knowledge, sources of - Descartes's Evil Demon, 102; Descartes's Wax, 108; Goodman's Grue, 144; Hume's Missing Shade of Blue, 112; Kant's *A Priori* Space, 116; Molyneux's Blind Man, 110; Plato's Equal Portions of Wood and Stone, 106. *See also* Empiricism; Rationalism.

language - Ayer's Robinson Crusoe, 96; James's Squirrel, 90; Putnam's Brain in a Vat, 62; Putnam's Twin Earth, 100; Quine's Gavagai, 98; Rorty's Antipodeans, 58; Wittgenstein's Games, 92; Wittgenstein's "S", 94

language, private - Ayer's Robinson Crusoe, 96; Wittgenstein's "S", 94

life and death - Brandt's Spelunkers, 156; Foot's Gas, 154; Hardin's Lifeboat, 210; Harris's Survival Lottery, 190; Jamieson and Regan's Terrorist Tank, 166; O'Neill's Lifeboat, 212; Parfit's Fission, 86; Price's *E. coli* John, 84; Regan's Lifeboat, 194; Thomson's Transplant Problem, 170; Thomson's Trolley Problem, 168

logic - The Barber Paradox, 136; Black's Two Spheres, 142; Frege's Other-Thinking Beings, 138; Goodman's Grue, 144; Hume's Constant Conjunction, 114; The Liar Paradox, 134; The Surprise Quiz, 140; Zeno's Achilles, 2

machines - Leibniz's Machine, 48; Searle's Chinese Room, 60; Turing's Imitation Game, 50

materialism - Berkeley's Impossibility of Conceiving the Unconceived, 6; Block's Chinese Nation, 56; Strawson's No-Space World, 10; Kirk and Squires's Zombies, 52

matter - Hobbes's Ship of Theseus, 68; Price's *E. coli* John, 84

meaning - Ayer's Robinson Crusoe, 96; James's Squirrel, 90; Putnam's Twin Earth, 100; Quine's Gavagai, 98; Wittgenstein's Games, 92; Wittgenstein's "S", 94

means and ends - Foot's Gas, 154; Sylvan's Last People, 186; Thomson's Transplant Problem, 170

mental states - Block's Chinese Nation, 56; Jackson's Mary, the Brilliant Color Scientist, 64; Leibniz's Machine, 48; Locke's Inverted Spectrum, 46; Nagel's Bat, 54; Putnam's Twin Earth, 100;

Rorty's Antipodeans, 58; Searle's Brain Replacement, 66

mind - Berkeley's Impossibility of Conceiving the Unconceived, 6; Block's Chinese Nation, 56; Jackson's Mary, the Brilliant Color Scientist, 64; Kirk and Squires's Zombies, 52; Leibniz's Machine, 48; Locke's Inverted Spectrum, 46; Nagel's Bat, 54; Putnam's Brain in a Vat, 64; Rorty's Antipodeans, 58; Searle's Brain Replacement, 66; Searle's Chinese Room, 60; Strawson's No-Space World, 10; Turing's Imitation Game, 50

mind/body - Block's Chinese Nation, 56; Jackson's Mary, the Brilliant Color Scientist, 64; Kirk and Squires's Zombies, 52; Leibniz's Machine, 48; Nagel's Bat, 54; Rorty's Antipodeans, 58; Searle's Brain Replacement, 66. *See also* Dualism.

moral absolutes - Jamieson and Regan's Chainsaw, 164

moral duties - Foot's Gas, 154; Hardin's Lifeboat, 210; O'Neill's Lifeboat, 212; Thomson's Trolley Problem, 168

moral obligations - Brandt's Spelunkers, 156; Hardin's Lifeboat, 210; O'Neill's Lifeboat, 212; The Routleys' Nuclear Train, 192

moral responsibility - Hardin's Lifeboat, 210; Hardin's Tragedy of the Commons, 204; James's Way Home, 18; Locke's Voluntary Prisoner, 16; O'Neill's Lifeboat, 212; The Routleys' Nuclear Train, 192; Sylvan's Last People, 186; Turing's Imitation Game, 50; Williams's Jim in South America, 158

motion - Zeno's Achilles, 2

nuclear development - The Routleys' Nuclear Train, 192

ontological argument (for the existence of a god) - Gaunilo's Lost Island, 28

other minds - Kirk and Squires's Zombies, 52; Locke's Inverted Spectrum, 46; Nagel's Bat, 54

overpopulation - Battin's Automatic Reversible Contraception, 198; Hardin's Lifeboat, 210

pain - Rorty's Antipodeans, 58

perception - Descartes's Evil Demon, 102; Descartes's Wax, 108; Hume's Missing Shade of Blue, 112; Jackson's Mary, the Brilliant Color Scientist, 64; Leibniz's Machine, 48; Locke's Inverted Spectrum, 46; Molyneux's Blind Man, 110

personal identity - *see* Identity, personal

personhood - Parfit's Teletransporter, 88; Perry's Divided Self, 82; Turing's Imitation Game, 50; Warren's Space Traveler, 182

physicalism - Block's Chinese Nation, 56; Kirk and Squires's Zombies, 52; Jackson's Mary, the Brilliant Color Scientist, 64; Searle's Brain Replacement, 66

pleasure - Donaldson's Equim, 172; Feinberg's Egoist, 162; Godwin's Fenelon, 148; Smart's Deluded Sadist, 152

potential people - Tooley's Kitten, 180; Warren's Space Explorer, 184

pragmatism - James' Squirrel, 90

prediction - Goldman's Book of Life, 22; Lyon's Card Predictor, 20

private language - *see* Language, private

property, private and common - Hardin's Tragedy of the Commons, 204; Locke's Acorns and Apples, 200; O'Neill's Lifeboat, 212; The Prisoner's Dilemma, 202

punishment - Alexander's Doomsday Machine, 214; Parfit's Nobelist, 218

race - Mills's Mr. Oreo, 220

rationalism - Descartes's Evil Demon, 102; Hume's Constant Conjunction, 114; Hume's Missing Shade of Blue, 112; Kant's *A Priori* Space, 116; Molyneux's Blind Man, 110

reality - Berkeley's Impossibility of Conceiving the Unconceived, 6; Lucretius's Spear, 4; Nietzche's Eternal Recurrence, 8; Quinton's Two-Space Myth, 12; Shoemaker's Time-Freezing World, 14; Strawson's No-Space World, 10; Zeno's Achilles, 2

reason - The Barber Paradox, 136; Frege's Other-Thinking Beings, 138; Goodman's Grue, 144; Hume's Constant Conjunction, 114; Kant's *A Priori* Space, 116; The Liar Paradox, 134; Mill's Chaotic World, 118; Molyneux's Blind Man, 110; The Surprise Quiz, 140

reliability - Lehrer's Mr. Truetemp, 132

reproductive issues - *see* Abortion; Contraception; Overpopulation

resurrection - Hick's Resurrected People, 38

rights - Brandt's Spelunkers, 156; Harris's Survival Lottery, 190; Nozick's Wilt Chamberlain, 208; O'Neill's Lifeboat, 212; Regan's Lifeboat, 194; Sylvan's Last People, 186; Thomson's Growing Child in a Tiny House, 176; Thomson's People-seeds, 178; Thomson's Violinist, 174; Tooley's Kitten, 180; Thomson's Transplant Problem, 170; Warren's Space Explorer, 184; Warren's Space Traveler, 182

robots - *see* Machines

self-defense - Harris's Survival Lottery, 190; Jamieson and Regan's Terrorist Tank, 166; Thomson's Growing Child in a Tiny House, 176; Thomson's People-seeds, 178

self-interest - Feinberg's Egoist, 162; Hardin's Tragedy of the Commons, 204; Marty's Two Shipwrecked Islanders, 216; Plato's Ring of Gyges, 146; The Prisoner's Dilemma, 202; Rawls's Veil of Ignorance, 206

sensory experience - Descartes's Evil Demon, 102; Descartes's Wax, 108; Hume's Constant Conjunction, 114;